# John McDonald's
# Maine Trivia

*by John McDonald*

Also from Islandport Press

*A Moose and a Lobster Walk into a Bar*
by John McDonald

*Down the Road a Piece: A Storyteller's Guide to Maine*
by John McDonald

*Bert and I . . . The Book*
by Marshall Dodge and Robert Bryan

*Headin' for the Rhubarb: A New Hampshire Dictionary*
by Rebecca Rule

*Live Free and Eat Pie!: A Storyteller's Guide to New Hampshire*
by Rebecca Rule

*Not Too Awful Bad: A Storyteller's Guide to Vermont*
by Leon Thompson

These and other great books are available at many book
resellers or online at www.islandportpress.com.

# JOHN MCDONALD'S
# MAINE TRIVIA

## A USEFUL GUIDE TO USELESS INFORMATION

*by John McDonald*

**ILLUSTRATED BY MARK RICKETTS**

ISLANDPORT PRESS

Islandport Press, Inc.
P.O. Box 10
Yarmouth, Maine 04096
www.islandportpress.com
books@islandportpress.com

ISBN: 978-1-934031-73-5
Library of Congress Card Number: 2011935468

Edited by Dean L. Lunt
Book jacket design by Karen F. Hoots / Hoots Design
Book design by Michelle A. Lunt / Islandport Press
Cover image of John McDonald by Dean L. Lunt

*To Ann*

# TABLE OF CONTENTS

# INTRODUCTION

I didn't start out to write a "trivia" book. To tell you the truth (a reckless activity storytellers should avoid), I can't remember now what kind of book I set out to write. But as Robert Frost says in "The Road Not Taken," we're always coming upon roads that diverge in the wood. And, here in Maine, when we come to a fork in the road, we take it.

When I started collecting Maine trivia, the working title for the book was *Useless Information: A User's Guide*. But my publisher, Dean, said, "John, how are we going to get people to shell out good money for a book with the word 'useless' printed right there on the cover, as bold as brass?"

What could I say?

Over the years I've thought about making a fortune writing either a cookbook or a diet book, known in the book business as big moneymakers. Year after year some of the most popular books on the market are one of the two—cookbooks or diet books. One will provide dozens of clever ways to fatten you up. The other will provide ways to slim you down. It's a perfect setup for publishers because they keep you going in circles—up and down—and it doesn't end until you croak.

Before you croak, of course, there are all kinds of books you can buy about "putting your affairs in order." There are even

books with instructions on planning your own funeral, complete with how-to advice on writing your own glowing obit and profound eulogy.

Some authors set out to write the ultimate self-improvement book—always a popular subject on bookstore shelves. Everyone can use a little improvement, right? Some can use a lot; just look around. With all the millions and millions of self-improvement books sold, wouldn't you think people would appear to be a little more improved than they are? That might be a subject for a future book.

Books about how to get filthy rich—and quickly—are always popular. *How I Went from Living on a Park Bench to Living at the Park Plaza* is a typical title. I thought about writing a get-rich-quick book. Then I wondered: How would it look to prospective book buyers if I showed up at a big book signing in my Subaru Outback? Not that I'm embarrassed by my Subaru; I'm not. It's a great car for Maine. But it's not the kind of car you'd expect a money expert to pull up in.

After some consideration I decided to leave all those subjects for another time.

I decided to write the book that follows, because, if used properly, I think it will help you lose weight, become a better person, make a lot of money, put your affairs in order, and plan your funeral.

Oh, and knowing its contents will also make you appear smarter than you really are.

So, buy this book, read it, and reap the results.

You can thank me later.

John McDonald
Otisfield, 2012
mainestoryteller@yahoo.com

# MAINE

**Q. ON WHAT DATE DID MAINE OFFICIALLY BECOME AN INDEPENDENT STATE?**

A. March 15, 1820.

**Q. MAINE WAS ADMITTED TO THE UNION AS THE TWENTY-THIRD STATE AS PART OF WHAT FAMOUS COMPROMISE?**

A. The Missouri Compromise. Maine was admitted as a free state and Missouri was allowed to enter as a slave state, to maintain a free-state, slave-state balance.

**Q. PRIOR TO STATEHOOD, THE SO-CALLED DISTRICT OF MAINE WAS PART OF WHAT OTHER STATE?**

A. Massachusetts. Apparently, the people of Massachusetts were so upset at losing Maine land that they've been buying the state back one house lot at a time ever since.

1

**Q. STATEHOOD DID NOT COME QUICKLY, OR EASILY. IN WHAT YEAR DID MAINERS FIRST VOTE ON WHETHER TO SEPARATE FROM MASSACHUSETTS?**

A. May 1792. It seems that after just a few short years under Massachusetts rule, Mainers threw up their arms and said, "Godfrey Daniel! And we thought the Brits were bad!" It was 1819, twenty-seven years later, before Mainers voted for the final time, approving separation, yet again. The final vote was 17,091 to 7,132.

AYUH,
THAT'S MIGHTY
INTERESTING,
JOHN!

*The term "crow flies" has nautical roots. In the days of sail (long before GPS and radar systems), mariners often brought caged crows on board their vessel. When sailors didn't know where the nearest land was, they would release a crow. Because crows are not water birds, they would fly straight toward the nearest land. The crow cages were kept high on the mast in what became known as the crow's nest.*

**Q. HOW MANY MILES OF COASTLINE DOES MAINE HAVE?**

A. It's 225 miles as a crow flies, but roughly 3,500 miles if you walk the entire length of Maine's picturesque coast along the high-water mark.

**Q. IN 1820, DELEGATES FROM MAINE'S EXISTING TOWNS MET IN PORTLAND'S FIRST PARISH CHURCH TO DRAFT THE REQUIRED STATE CONSTITUTION. WHAT NAME OTHER THAN MAINE WAS CONSIDERED FOR THE NEW STATE?**

A. Columbus. According to *Maine: A Narrative History*, Daniel Cony of Augusta was one of the people who favored the name Columbus.

**Q. WHAT WAS MAINE'S POPULATION IN 2010?**

A. 1.328 million.

**Q. WHERE DOES MAINE RANK AMONG THE FIFTY STATES IN TERMS OF POPULATION?**

A. Forty-first.

**Q. IN WHAT CENSUS YEAR DID THE POPULATION OF MAINE FIRST SURPASS 500,000?**

A. 1840 (501,793).

**Q. HOW MANY LAKES AND PONDS CAN BE FOUND IN MAINE?**

A. Roughly 6,000. If you want the exact number, count them yourself. We have better things to do.

**Q. MAINE'S OFFICIAL MOTTO IS "DIRIGO." WHAT DOES THE WORD MEAN?**

A. Dirigo is Latin for "I direct" or "I lead." Notice that our motto doesn't include a destination? If you're heading north on the Maine Turnpike you'll be directed to the York tollbooths. If you're heading south on the turnpike you'll be led to a fleecing from our New Hampshire neighbors at the Hampton tollbooth.

**Q. WHAT CITY IS THE CAPITAL OF MAINE?**

A. Augusta (population: 19,136).

**Q. AUGUSTA HAS NOT ALWAYS BEEN THE STATE CAPITAL. WHAT OTHER CITY ONCE SERVED AS THE CAPITAL OF MAINE?**

A. Portland served as Maine's capital, from 1820 to 1832.

**Q. I ᴋɴᴏᴡ ᴡʜᴀᴛ ʏᴏᴜ'ʀᴇ ᴛʜɪɴᴋɪɴɢ: Pᴏʀᴛʟᴀɴᴅ? Rᴇᴀʟʟʏ? Wᴇʀᴇ ᴛʜᴇ Mᴀɪɴᴇʀs ᴡʜᴏ ᴄʜᴏsᴇ Pᴏʀᴛʟᴀɴᴅ ᴀs ᴛʜᴇ sᴛᴀᴛᴇ's ғɪʀsᴛ ᴄᴀᴘɪᴛᴀʟ sᴇʀɪ-ᴏᴜs? Wᴇʀᴇ ᴛʜᴇʏ ᴅʀᴜɴᴋ?**

A. I have no good answer. I sincerely believe they just wanted to see if other Mainers were paying attention. Apparently, other Mainers were off at a nineteenth-century yard sale or something and let Portland stand as capital for twelve years.

**Q. Wʜᴀᴛ ɪs ᴛʜᴇ Mᴀɪɴᴇ sᴛᴀᴛᴇ ғʟᴏᴡᴇʀ?**

A. Pinecone and tassel. Some don't even realize this is a flower, and it certainly doesn't show up in many bridal bou- quets (or any other bou- quets, for that matter). But we love it—so there!

**Q. Hᴏᴡ ᴍᴀɴʏ ᴄᴏᴜɴᴛɪᴇs ᴀʀᴇ ʟᴏᴄᴀᴛᴇᴅ ɪɴ Mᴀɪɴᴇ?**

A. Maine has 16 counties.

**Q. Sᴘᴇᴀᴋɪɴɢ ᴏғ Mᴀɪɴᴇ ᴄᴏᴜɴᴛɪᴇs, ɪɴɴᴜᴍᴇʀᴀʙʟᴇ Mᴀɪɴᴇ sᴄʜᴏᴏʟ-ᴄʜɪʟᴅʀᴇɴ ᴏᴠᴇʀ ᴛʜᴇ ʏᴇᴀʀs ʜᴀᴠᴇ ʟᴇᴀʀɴᴇᴅ ᴛʜᴇ ɴᴀᴍᴇs ᴏғ ᴛʜᴇ sɪxᴛᴇᴇɴ ᴄᴏᴜɴᴛɪᴇs ʙʏ ᴍᴇᴍᴏʀɪᴢɪɴɢ ᴛʜᴇ "Mᴀɪɴᴇ Cᴏᴜɴᴛʏ Sᴏɴɢ." Tᴏ ᴡʜᴀᴛ ᴛᴜɴᴇ ɪs ᴛʜᴀᴛ sᴏɴɢ sᴜɴɢ?**

A. "Yankee Doodle Dandy."

**Q. NAME ALL SIXTEEN COUNTIES. PLEASE, NO NEED TO SING 'EM.**

A. They are:

1. Cumberland
2. Franklin
3. Piscataquis
4. Somerset
5. Aroostook
6. Androscoggin
7. Sagadahoc
8. Kennebec
9. Lincoln
10. Knox
11. Hancock
12. Waldo
13. Washington
14. York
15. Oxford
16. Penobscot

**Q. SEVEN OF MAINE'S SIXTEEN COUNTIES WERE FOUNDED AFTER STATEHOOD. NAME THEM.**

A. Androscoggin, Aroostook, Franklin, Knox, Piscataquis, Sagadahoc, and Waldo.

**Q. WHAT IS THE STATE'S OFFICIAL NICKNAME?**

A. The Pine Tree State—which is just so much better than The Coffee Brandy State or The Scratch-Ticket State, which I believe were two of the original suggestions.

**Q. What slogan began appearing on Maine license plates in 1936?**

A. Vacationland.

**Q. In 2012, what is the official slogan of the state's tourism industry?**

A. "Get lost!" No, no, that's actually my personal slogan. It's really "Maine—the way life should be."

**Q. What wise guy suggested that Maine's motto should be: "Cold, but damp!"?**

A. Humorist Dave Barry.

**Q. What is the official Maine pastime?**

A. Going to yard sales. Okay, I made that up; there is no official state pastime.

**Q. How many area codes does Maine have?**

A. One.

**Q. What is the state's area code?**

A. 207.

**Q. What is Maine's smallest county when measured by land area?**

A. Sagadahoc County (254 square miles).

*The town of Franklin is in Knox County, not Franklin County; the town of Knox is in Waldo County, not Knox County; the town of Lincoln is in Penobscot County, not Lincoln County; the town of Penobscot is in Hancock County, not Penobscot County; and the town of Washington is in Knox County, not Washington County.*

**Q. NAME MAINE'S FIVE LARGEST CITIES, IN TERMS OF POPULATION. BONUS POINTS IF YOU CAN NAME THEM IN ORDER FROM LARGEST TO SMALLEST, ACCORDING TO THE 2010 CENSUS.**

A. Portland (66,194), Lewiston (36,592), Bangor (33,039), South Portland (25,002), Auburn (23,055).

**Q. WHAT IS MAINE'S SMALLEST CITY IN TERMS OF POPULATION?**

A. Eastport (1,640).

**Q. WHO WAS MAINE'S FIRST GOVERNOR?**

A. William King. King—a Bath merchant who is sometimes called the "Father of the State of Maine"—helped lead the movement that resulted in Maine's separation from Massachusetts.

**Q. WHERE DOES THE MAINE TURNPIKE BEGIN AND END?**

A. The turnpike, dedicated in 1955, runs from Kittery to Augusta.

**Q. WHAT IS THE STATE HERB?**

A. Wintergreen.

**Q. WHAT IS THE STATE GEMSTONE?**

A. Tourmaline. Mount Mica, located near Paris in Oxford County, was the first source of tourmaline in the United States, and became the first gem mine in America as well. Mount Mica was discovered in 1821 by two young men walking through the area, Ezekiel Holmes and Elijah Hamlin. Elijah Hamlin, later one of the founders of the Bangor Savings Bank, was the brother of Hannibal Hamlin, who would serve as Abraham Lincoln's first vice president.

**Q. WHAT IS THE STATE TREE?**

A. Eastern white pine. This pine can grow from 75 to 150 feet tall. The white pine helped establish Maine in the nineteenth century as the lumber capital of the world and the predominant shipbuilding state.

**Q. WHAT PERCENTAGE OF MAINE IS FORESTED?**

A. Roughly 90 percent of Maine land is covered by trees.

AYUH, THAT'S MIGHTY INTERESTING, JOHN!

Maine is the only state that is bordered by only one other state.

Unfortunately for us, the one state we border is New Hampshire. Just kidding! All seriousness aside, we love our "Live Free or Die!" neighbors. However, there is always some bickering about exactly where the border lies. I remember a few years ago, I heard a team of surveyors was hired by Maine and New Hampshire to try to set the border once and for all.

One day they were working in Oxford County, and after spending a day going through swamps and fields and pucker-brush, they realized that a farm on the border was not in Maine at all, but was actually in New Hampshire.

One of the surveyors was given the task of telling the owner the news. The surveyor fella was a little concerned because he didn't know how the farm's owner would take to being told his farm had just moved from one state to another. He walked up to the farmhouse, called "hello" a few times, and finally, an elderly gentleman came to the door.

"Sir," he said, "I'm with the survey team, straightening out the border here, and after surveying through your farm, we discovered that your place isn't in Maine at all—it's actually in New Hampshire."

The old man looked a little stunned at first, but then said, "Well, thank you, young fella, for that news, and thank the good Lord, too. You know, I was just sitting here wondering how I was going to make it through another Maine winter."

**Q. WHAT IS THE STATE ANIMAL?**

A. Moose. A moose can grow up to seven feet tall at the shoulder and can weigh more than 1,500 pounds. A typical moose lives fifteen to twenty-five years. Virtually all tourists come to Maine to see a moose, eat a lobster, and photograph a lighthouse.

**Q. WHAT IS THE STATE BERRY?**

A. The blueberry, of course. Duh.

**Q. WHAT IS MAINE'S LARGEST LAKE?**

A. Moosehead Lake (74,890 acres). Sebago Lake (28,771 acres) is a distant second, followed by Chesuncook Lake (23,070 acres).

**Q. WHAT IS MAINE'S SMALLEST LAKE?**

A. We're still trying to find it. We'll let you know when we do.

**Q. WHAT IS MAINE'S HIGHEST MOUNTAIN?**

A. Katahdin (5,267 feet).

**Q. NAME MAINE'S FIVE HIGHEST MOUNTAINS.**

A. Katahdin (5,267 feet), Sugarloaf (4,237 feet), Old Speck (4,180 feet), Crocker Mountain (4,168 feet), Bigelow Mountain (4,150 feet).

**Q. WHERE WOULD YOU GO IN MAINE FOR A BOWL OF MANHATTAN CLAM CHOWDER?**

A. Oh, please! This is another trick question. Nowhere! There's no place we know of—and certainly no place I would actually tell you about—that serves that type of chowder in Maine. You'll have to go back to Manhattan if you insist on eating the stuff. When Perley Leighton was served his first and only bowl of Manhattan clam chowder, he asked the waitress what bled in there. But if you decide to leave on account of our chowder, please, buy some Maine souvenirs and books before you go. All major credit cards accepted. Thanks.

**Q. WHAT IS THE NICKNAME FOR AROOSTOOK COUNTY?**

A. Simply, "The County." At 6,453 square miles, not only is it Maine's largest county, but it's also larger than Connecticut and Rhode Island combined. Granted, there may be only a few places smaller than L'il Rhody, but Aroostook's size is still pretty impressive.

**Q. MAINE IS WORLD-RENOWNED FOR ITS LOBSTER. HOW MANY POUNDS OF LOBSTER ARE CAUGHT OFF THE COAST OF MAINE EACH YEAR?**

A. In 2011, Maine lobstermen and lobsterwomen caught more than 100 million pounds of the famous crustacean, surpassing the previous record of 94.7 million pounds, set in 2010. That translates into a lot of butter and lobster-bib sales as well.

**Q. WHAT PERCENTAGE OF THE NATION'S WILD BLUEBERRY SUPPLY IS HARVESTED IN MAINE?**

A. Maine has more than 60,000 acres of wild blueberry fields and raises roughly 98 to 99 percent of our country's wild blueberry crop.

**Q. WHAT TWO PROFESSIONS ARE DEPICTED ON THE MAINE STATE SEAL?**

A. There were no Cumberland Farms, McDonald's, or casino jobs back in 1820 when the seal was designed, so designers went with a farmer on the left side of the seal and a mariner on the right—the two most common professions in the early nineteenth century.

**Q. WHAT IS THE LONGEST RIVER IN MAINE?**

A. The St. John River (418 miles). However, the river—which forms the northern boundary between Maine and Canada—is not entirely in Maine. The state's second-longest river, and the longest river located entirely in the state of Maine, is the Penobscot River, which, including the river's west and south branches, is 264 miles long.

**Q. WHAT IS THE MOST OVERUSED PLACE NAME IN MAINE?**

A. "Mud Pond" wins hands down, with sixty-five. But the fun doesn't end with Mud Ponds. Maine also has twelve Mud Brooks and fourteen Mud Lakes. Those names would suggest that there's a lot of mud here in Maine. The names also indicate a lack of originality in our state's "place names" department. I want to know why a state that's as rocky as Maine has sixty-five Mud Ponds and only eighteen Stony Brooks.

**Q. What five rivers meet in Merrymeeting Bay? ("Meet"—get it?)**

A. The Kennebec, Androscoggin, Cathance, Abagadasset, and Eastern. As they say in Brunswick, the more rivers, the merrier the meeting.

**Q. What is the easternmost point of land in the United States?**

A. West Quoddy Head. Go figure. East Quoddy Head is in New Brunswick, Canada.

**Q. What is Maine's largest island?**

A. Mount Desert Island. At 108 square miles, MDI, as it's known locally, is the second-largest island along the nation's East Coast, and the sixth-largest island in the contiguous United States.

AYUH, THAT'S MIGHTY INTERESTING, JOHN!

*One sure way to tell if someone is "local" or "from away" is the way they pronounce the name of Maine's largest island. If they pronounce the name as if it were an actual "desert," as in sand, sand everywhere, they are from away. If they pronounce it as if it were a treat, such as a delicious Maine blueberry pie eaten after a meal, as in "dessert," they are local (or at least doing a good job of faking it).*

**Q. Bangor was known by what two nicknames in the nineteenth century?**

A. Queen City of the East and Lumber Capital of the World.

**Q. HOW BIG IS MAINE?**

A. 33,215 square miles. Maine seems small when compared to Alaska's 656,425 square miles, but it's still nearly as large as the other five New England states—combined!

**Q. EVERY STATE HAS DISORGANIZED MUNICIPALITIES AND GOVERN-MENTS, BUT MAINE ALSO HAS AREAS CALLED "UNORGANIZED TERRITO-RIES." HOW MUCH OF MAINE IS "UNORGANIZED"?**

A. They say it's 44 percent. The percentage of "disorganized places" is anybody's guess.

**Q. IN 2003, MAINE BECAME THE FIRST STATE TO GIVE THESE TO ALL SEVENTH-GRADE STUDENTS.**

A. Laptop computers.

**Q. ARE THERE ANY PEAT BOGS IN MAINE?**

A. I guess, probl'y; at last count there were 700,000 acres of them.

**Q. WHAT TWO OCEAN CURRENTS MEET THIRTY MILES OFF THE MAINE COAST?**

A. The Gulf Stream and the Arctic Current.

**Q. HOW LONG IS MAINE AT ITS WIDEST POINT?**

A. 320 miles.

**Q. MAINE HAS ONLY ONE SYLLABLE IN ITS NAME. WHAT OTHER STATE (OR STATES) ALSO HAVE ONLY ONE SYLLABLE?**

A. None.

**Q. WHAT IS ONE THING THAT CAN BE SAID ABOUT AUGUSTA THAT YOU CAN'T SAY ABOUT ANY OTHER STATE CAPITAL?**

A. Hey! That's not very nice. I can't write that in this wholesome book. The correct answer is that Augusta is the easternmost capital city in the United States. Okay, it's not a big deal, but it's something.

**Q: WHERE DID MAINE GET ITS NAME?**

A: Who knows? It's a good question, and I wish I could answer it, but I can't. The fact is, no one knows for sure where the name "Maine" came from. All we can do here is offer a list of possible explanations and ask you to pick the one you like best.

The first known record of the name "Maine," referring to the land area that eventually became our country's twenty-third state, appears in a land charter dated August 10, 1622, which gave large tracts of land to English Navy veterans Sir Fernando Gorges and Captain John Mason. The charter says Gorges and Mason "intend to name the tract: The Province of Maine." Mason had served in the Royal Navy, in the Orkney Islands off Scotland (where the principal island is called Mainland), so some think Maine's name came from that connection. Others think Maine is named after the former French province of Maine.

It's more likely that two veterans of His Majesty's Royal Navy would go with a Scottish place name over a name from France. Not that they'd ever do anything shamelessly "political," but Maine's legislature, in 2001, adopted a resolution establishing Franco-American Day, boldly stating in a proclamation that Maine was named after the former French province of Maine.

In 1623, the English naval captain Christopher Levett, while exploring the New England coast, wrote in his log: "The first place I set my foote upon in New England was the Isle of Shoulds, being Ilands [sic] in the sea, above two Leagues from Mayne."

Wherever the name or spelling came from, the name "Maine" was settled in 1665 when His Majesty's Commissioners ordered that the "Province of Maine" be entered from then on in official records.

**Q: WHAT IS THE OFFICIAL STATE TREAT?**

A: The Whoopie Pie. Originally, the Whoopie Pie was going to be the state's official dessert, but the blueberry crowd didn't take kindly to that notion. And then, to further confuse matters, some lawmakers were concerned about glorifying a snack food given the growing issue of childhood obesity. So, the word "dessert" was changed to "treat," and the blueberry pie was designated the official dessert. Win-win!

**Q. WHY SHOULD YOU NEVER ORDER THE SOUP DU JOUR AT A MAINE RESTAURANT?**

A. Because you never know from one day to the next what it's going to be. LOL! (or is LOL a little too trendy?)

**Q. CAN YOU BELIEVE WE SHARE OUR STATE BIRD WITH THE COMMONWEALTH OF MASSACHUSETTS? WE DIDN'T BELIEVE IT EITHER. WHAT IS THE BIRD WE SHARE WITH THE BAY STATE?**

A. The black-capped chickadee. It's also the provincial bird of New Brunswick, which is fine.

**Q. WHAT IS MAINE'S STATE INSECT?**

A. The honeybee. Yes, we've all heard the jokes about either the mosquito or the blackfly being our "official" state insect, but those stories are not true.

**Q. WHAT IS MAINE'S OFFICIAL FISH?**

A. The landlocked salmon. The average landlocked salmon is sixteen to eighteen inches long and weighs one to one and a half pounds. However, it's not uncommon for a salmon to weigh three to five pounds.

According to the Maine Department of Inland Fisheries and Wildlife, prior to 1868, landlocked salmon were only found in four Maine river basins: the St. Croix, including West Grand Lake in Washington County; the Union, including Green Lake in Hancock County; the Penobscot, including Sebec Lake in Piscataquis County; and the Presumpscot, including Sebago Lake, in Cumberland County. Today, landlocked salmon can be found in significant numbers in more than 175 lakes. They can also be found in more than 125 additional waters. Landlocked salmon also provide good fisheries in 44 rivers and streams, totaling about 290 miles.

**Q. THE "STATE OF MAINE SONG" WAS WRITTEN BY ROGER VINTON SNOW. PLEASE RECITE THE OPENING LINES:**

> A: *Grand State of Maine,*
> *proudly we sing*
> *To tell your glories to the land,*
> *To shout your praises till the echoes ring.*
> *Should fate unkind*

*send us to roam,*
*The scent of the fragrant pines,*
*the tang of the salty sea*
*Will call us home.*

*CHORUS:*
*Oh, Pine Tree State,*
*Your woods, fields, and hills,*
*Your lakes, streams, and rockbound coast*
*Will ever fill our hearts with thrills,*
*And tho' we seek far and wide*
*Our search will be in vain,*
*To find a fairer spot on earth*
*Than Maine! Maine! Maine!*

Okay, so he was no Cole Porter, but at least he tried. How many Maine songs have you written lately?

**Q. WHAT IS THE STATE CAT?**

A. Maine coon. And a beautiful cat it is. Trust me, people can become very attached to a special Maine coon.

Speaking of cats, I once heard a story about Wilbur Beal, who, after many exhausting years of nonstop clamming, blueberry picking, and fishing, decided to actually leave Washington County and take a vacation. There were tons of places in Maine he wanted to see but had only read about in magazines, places like Island Falls and Jackman and Madawaska. He was worried about leaving his Maine coon cat behind, but he really did need a vacation.

So off he went. He left his brother Liston to look after things, including his beloved Maine coon. The first day he got to Caribou, he checked into a hotel and called back home to see how things were going.

Liston answered the phone.

"How's everything back home, Liston?" Wilbur asked, getting right to the point.

"Oh, things is okay, I guess," Liston said.

Then, after a short pause, he added, "Oh, by the way—your cat's dead."

The cat that Liston so bluntly reported dead was no ordinary cat. It happened to be a prized Maine coon, and was probably the most valuable thing Wilbur owned.

Wilbur was some upset by Liston's report of the cat's demise. He said, "I just want you to know, Liston, that you've probably ruined my entire vacation, giving me such bad news on the first day out."

Liston said he was sorry, but he thought Wilbur should know about his cat.

"Of course I should know," said Wilbur. "But when someone's going to be on the road a week or two, and they call back the first night to see how things are, you don't hit 'em right between the eyes with the bad news all at once."

"Then how should I have told you?" Liston asked, all flustered.

"You should say something like: 'Your cat's up on the roof, and she won't come down,' " said Wilbur. "That way I don't worry, seeing I know she's been on the roof before."

Wilbur continued: "The next night when I call, you say, 'We got your cat off the roof, but we dropped her on her back and damaged her vertebrae.' A little more serious, but I still think she'll pull through.

"When I call the next night, you say, 'Your cat's at the vet's, in serious condition.' The next night, you tell me she's in a coma. And on the last night, you say my cat died quietly in her sleep. That's how you break bad news to someone who's going to be on vacation for two weeks. Understand?"

"Yes," Liston said, all apologetic and shameful.

Next day, Wilbur continued along on his vacation, driving up to Fort Kent. After a good supper at the local country store, Wilbur went back to his motel and called home to check on things. Again, Liston answered.

"How are things back home?" Wilbur asked.

"Oh, things is okay, I guess," said Liston.

"That's good," said a relieved Wilbur. "And how's Mother?"

"Well, she's up on the roof," Liston said, "and she won't come down."

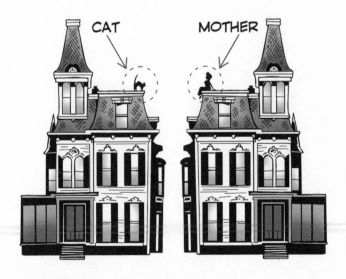

**Q. WHO DESCRIBED MAINE IN THESE WORDS?**

> *All I could see from where I stood*
> *was three long mountains and a wood*
> *I turned and looked the other way*
> *and saw three islands in a bay.*

A. American poet and Camden native Edna St. Vincent Millay.

# HISTORY AND POLITICS

**Q. WHAT PORTLAND NATIVE AND POWERFUL NINETEENTH-CENTURY NATIONAL POLITICIAN FAMOUSLY SAID ABOUT THE TWO-PARTY POLITICAL SYSTEM: "THE BEST SYSTEM IS TO HAVE ONE PARTY GOVERN AND THE OTHER PARTY WATCH."**

A. Thomas Brackett "Czar" Reed (1839–1902), who served as Speaker of the U.S. House of Representatives from 1889 to 1891, and from 1895 to 1899.

**Q. GENERAL ULYSSES S. GRANT CHOSE THIS BREWER NATIVE AND MAINE GENERAL TO ACCEPT THE SWORD OF SURRENDER FROM ROBERT E. LEE AT APPOMATTOX COURT HOUSE IN 1865.**

A. Joshua Lawrence Chamberlain (1828–1914). Chamberlain went on to serve as president of Bowdoin College and as governor of Maine. He was also the only officer during the war to receive a battlefield promotion to general.

**Q. WHILE ACCEPTING THE SWORD OF SURRENDER FROM GENERAL LEE'S ARMY, WHAT DID CHAMBERLAIN FAMOUSLY TELL HIS MEN TO DO?**

A. As Confederate soldiers marched to surrender their arms and colors, Chamberlain ordered his men to come to attention and "carry arms" as a show of respect. Chamberlain later described the scene: "All the while on our part not a sound of trumpet or drum, not a cheer, nor a word nor motion of man, but awful stillness as if it were the passing of the dead."

*On the second day of the Battle of Gettysburg, Confederate forces began attacking the Union left flank. Chamberlain and the 20th Maine were sent to defend the southern slope of Little Round Top at the far left end of the entire Union line. From a strategic standpoint, the small hill was extremely important, and Chamberlain knew the 20th Maine had to hold the Union left at all costs. The 15th Alabama Infantry regiment repeatedly attacked Chamberlain's position until the 20th Maine was almost doubled back upon itself. After suffering casualties and with ammunition running low, Chamberlain ordered his left wing to initiate a bayonet charge. The 20th Maine charged down the hill, with the left wing wheeling continually to make the charging line swing like a hinge, thus creating a simultaneous frontal assault and flanking maneuver, capturing 101 of the Confederate soldiers and successfully saving the flank.*

**Q. WHAT PULITZER PRIZE–WINNING HISTORICAL NOVEL, WHICH FOCUSED PRIMARILY ON THE FOUR DAYS OF THE BATTLE OF GETTYSBURG, IS CREDITED WITH REVIVING INTEREST IN THE HEROICS OF CHAMBERLAIN AND THE 20TH MAINE AT LITTLE ROUND TOP?**

A. *The Killer Angels* by Michael Shaara was awarded the Pulitzer Prize for Fiction in 1975.

*Portland mayor James Phinney Baxter (1831–1921) may have been Maine's most prolific historical writer and editor. Baxter edited twenty volumes of the twenty-four-volume work* Documentary History of the State of Maine, *which isn't exactly a page-turner, but is still an important historical work. Baxter was also the driving force behind Portland's tree-lined Baxter Boulevard and the father of Percival Baxter, Maine's fifty-third governor and creator of Baxter State Park.*

**Q. WHAT MAINE MAN SERVED AS ABRAHAM LINCOLN'S FIRST VICE PRESIDENT?**

A. If you have been reading carefully, you'll already know this: Hannibal Hamlin (1809–1891). Hamlin, a native of Paris Hill, was a fiery antislavery politician and prominent U.S. senator who famously left the Democratic Party over its pro-slavery stance. He caused a national sensation when he joined the new Republican Party. He served as the first Republican vice president. For Lincoln's second term, politician Andrew Johnson—who was more sympathetic to the South—was chosen to replace Hamlin. Hamlin returned to the Senate for two six-year terms after he served as vice president.

Hamlin's vice presidency helped usher in a half-century of amazing national influence for the Maine Republican Party. Starting with Hamlin, Maine Republicans occupied the offices of vice president, secretary of the treasury (twice), secretary of state, president pro tempore of the United States Senate, Speaker of the United States House of Representatives (twice), and fielded a national presidential candidate in James G. Blaine.

**Q: WHAT IS THE NAME OF THE MAINE GOVERNOR'S MANSION?**

A. The Blaine House.

**Q. FOR WHOM IS THE STATE'S GOVERNOR'S MANSION NAMED?**

A. James G. Blaine, one of Maine's most famous and successful politicians. Although he hated to admit it in public here in Maine, James G. Blaine was actually from away. He was born in 1830 in the sleepy little town of West Brownsville, Pennsylvania. Blaine came up here to Maine in 1854 when he was hired as editor of the *Kennebec Journal* in Augusta. Later, in what some would consider a step up (and others would consider a step down), he moved to Portland to become editor of the *Portland Advertiser*. In 1859, Blaine was elected to the Maine House of Representatives, where he served three years, the last year as Speaker. Then he moved on to Congress as a representative from Maine. He had done so well as Speaker of the Maine House that his colleagues in Congress elected him Speaker there as well.

In 1876, he resigned from Congress and ran unsuccessfully for the Republican nomination for president. He ran for the same nomination four years later and lost once again. Third time being the charm—at least for the presidential nomination— Blaine became the Republican candidate for president in 1884, but he managed to lose the election, anyway, to Grover Cleveland. But he came so close. How close? Well, he lost New York State, and thereby the election, by about one thousand votes.

Many people, including Blaine, thought he lost because of remarks made in New York on the eve of the election by Reverend Samuel D. Burchard, supposedly on Blaine's behalf. In an emotional speech, the teetotaling, anti-Catholic Burchard referred to the opposing party—the Democrats—as the party of ". . . Rum, Romanism and Rebellion!" The speech got lots of people all riled up. Despite the fact that this occurred well before talk radio, *Crossfire*, *Hardball*, and iPhones, the reverend's words spread like wildfire throughout New York's immigrant population, offending many Irish Catholics in the process. In the remaining hours of the campaign Blaine reminded New York voters that his own mother was a Catholic, but it was not enough. Blaine died in Washington in 1893, and his body was later brought back to Augusta, where he was buried in Blaine Memorial Park.

AYUH, THAT'S MIGHTY INTERESTING, JOHN!

*The 1884 campaign between Blaine and Grover Cleveland became famous for two nasty campaign slogans, one aimed at each candidate. Cleveland supporters often chanted, "James G. Blaine, James G. Blaine, the continental liar from the State of Maine," while Blaine supporters, after discovering reports that Cleveland had fathered an illegitimate child, chanted, "Ma, Ma, where's my pa?" After Cleveland won the election, the ending of the chant became, "Gone to the White House, ha, ha, ha." Yes, I suppose Longfellow could have written better slogans, but he never offered his services to either candidate.*

**Q. IN WHAT MAINE TOWN WAS AMERICA'S FIRST SARDINE CANNERY BUILT?**

A. Eastport. The first U.S. sardine cannery opened there in 1875, when a New York businessman set up the Eagle Preserved Fish Company.

**Q. IN THE MIDDLE OF PORTLAND HARBOR SITS A PILE OF SLOWLY SINKING GRANITE STONES NAMED "FORT GORGES." FOR WHOM IS THE FORT NAMED?**

A. Sir Ferdinando Gorges. Gorges was an early entrepreneur in the English colonies, considered by some to be "the father of English colonization in the New World." In 1622, he and business partner John Mason received a land patent for the Province of Maine from the Plymouth Council for New England. Gorges was a shareholder in the Plymouth Company, and also helped to fund the failed Popham Colony on the Kennebec River.

**Q. WHO WAS THE LAST PERSON EXECUTED IN MAINE?**

A. Daniel Wilkinson. On November 21, 1885, Wilkinson was hanged for the murder of a Bath police officer after a burglary in Bath.

**Q. WHERE AND WHEN DID THE FIRST EUROPEANS SETTLE IN MAINE?**

A. In 1604, a French party that included the Sieur de Monts and famed explorer Samuel de Champlain settled on a small island in the St. Croix River, midway between Maine and New Brunswick. It was a poor location. Half of the settlement died the first winter, and the colony was abandoned the following spring.

**Q. WHO NAMED MOUNT DESERT ISLAND?**

A. Samuel de Champlain. As he was sailing past the island in the early 1600s, he looked at the island's barren mountains and called it *L'Isle des Monts-desert*.

*The English civil war of the 1640s played an important role in Maine's history. The distraction of the civil war in England allowed Massachusetts to gain control of Maine as early as 1652. Charles II interrupted that control for a while, but then, in 1677, Massachusetts purchased all claims of the Gorges family for 1,250 pounds. We can only imagine what Maine's history would have been like if Charles hadn't been driven from the throne and William and Mary had taken over. In 1691, they granted Massachusetts a new charter that only confirmed the Commonwealth's title to all of Maine. A lot like it is today.*

AYUH, THAT'S MIGHTY INTERESTING, JOHN!

**Q. IN WHAT YEAR WAS SLAVERY ABOLISHED IN MAINE?**

A. 1788.

**Q. "REMEMBER THE *MAINE*" BECAME THE BATTLE CRY OF THE SPANISH-AMERICAN WAR. TO WHAT INCIDENT IS IT REFERRING?**

A. In 1898, the battleship *Maine* was blown up in Havana Harbor.

**Q. ACCORDING TO SOME, WHICH EUROPEANS WERE POSSIBLY THE FIRST TO VISIT MAINE, AROUND AD 1000?**

A. Norse sailors led by Leif Erikson. It just may be that the Vikings were the first to visit Maine, but if so, they didn't realize they'd discovered the New World; they just thought they'd found a great fishing spot. So, like all good fishermen, they didn't tell anyone where it was.

**Q. GIVEN THE LACK OF ACTUAL EVIDENCE TO SUPPORT A VISIT TO MAINE BY VIKINGS, WHO IS IDENTIFIED AS THE FIRST EUROPEAN TO EXPLORE THE COAST OF MAINE?**

A. Giovanni da Verrazzano, an Italian explorer sailing for France, in 1524.

**Q. WHEN AND WHERE WAS THE FIRST BRITISH COLONY ESTABLISHED IN MAINE?**

A. In 1607, just a few short months after the more-famous colony in Jamestown, Virginia, was established. Sir George Popham and his second-in-command, Raleigh Gilbert, established the Popham Colony in what is now Phippsburg. They arrived on the *Gift of God* in August, followed shortly by the *Mary and John*. The 120 colonists built Fort St. George. A map made that October shows eighteen buildings. Roughly half of the colonists returned home that December, but the rest stayed the winter. Late the following summer of 1608, the entire colony returned to England. Apparently merry olde England looked a lot merrier after a Maine winter.

**Q. WHILE THE POPHAM COLONY WAS SHORT-LIVED, IT IS FAMOUS FOR BUILDING WHAT?**

A. The *Virginia*, a thirty-ton pinnace that was the first vessel built by Europeans in the New World. It was built at the mouth of the Kennebec River by the colonists of that unsuccessful settlement. They built the ship in part to prove the settlement could survive as a shipbuilding settlement. In the summer of 1608, when all the remaining colonists returned to England, some sailed in the *Mary and John* and the rest in the newly built *Virginia*. The *Virginia* would make at least one more transatlantic trip, helping to supply the Jamestown Colony in 1609.

**Q. IN 1851, THE SO-CALLED "MAINE LAW" WAS PASSED, MAKING MAINE THE FIRST STATE IN THE NATION TO BAN THE MANUFACTURE, SALE, AND POSSESSION OF WHAT PRODUCT?**

A. Alcohol. The law was temporarily repealed in 1856, but essentially Maine was "dry" from 1851 until Prohibition ended in 1933.

**Q. WHAT FAMOUS PORTLAND MAYOR WAS CONSIDERED THE "FATHER OF PROHIBITION" AND WAS THE DRIVING FORCE BEHIND THE MAINE LAW?**

A. Neal Dow. Dow was raised a Quaker and served as a city fireman and mayor of Portland. He even ran for president on the Prohibition Party ticket in 1880. He didn't win.

*Not only was Neal Dow the force behind Prohibition, but he also served as a general during the Civil War. Dow was wounded and held captive by Confederate forces for several months. Eventually, he was exchanged for William Henry Fitzhugh Lee, son of General Robert E. Lee.*

**Q. WHAT MAINE FORT SERVED AS THE STAGING GROUND FOR BENEDICT ARNOLD'S FAILED ATTEMPT TO ATTACK QUEBEC IN 1775?**

A. Fort Western on the Kennebec River in Augusta.

**Q. IN WHAT YEAR WAS MAINE'S FIRST NEWSPAPER PUBLISHED?**

A. Benjamin Titcomb Jr. and his business partner Thomas B. Wait published *The Falmouth Gazette* in 1785. Interestingly enough, Marden's ran the first ad. Nah, just kidding; it was actually Reny's.

**Q. DURING THE REVOLUTIONARY WAR, PORTLAND WAS KNOWN BY WHAT NAME?**

A. Falmouth.

**Q. IN 1866, A FAMOUS FIRE DESTROYED MUCH OF THIS CITY, LEAVING THOUSANDS HOMELESS.**

A. Portland. Starting on July 4, the fire devastated Portland, destroying 1,500 homes, more than 100 manufacturers, and dozens of retail businesses and public buildings, including 4 schools. It left more than 10,000 people homeless. The great Henry Wadsworth Longfellow, whose house was spared, wrote: "I've been in Portland since the fire. Desolation! Desolation! Desolation! It reminds me of Pompeii."

**Q. IN 1911, ANOTHER FAMOUS FIRE DEVASTATED THE DOWNTOWN SECTION OF WHAT CITY.**

A. Bangor. The Great Fire of 1911 wiped out nearly half of downtown Bangor. The fire burned fifty-five acres of the city, destroying 267 buildings and damaging 100 more. More than 260 buildings were completely gone, including six churches, a synagogue, the high school, the post office, the library, and the historical society. Dozens and dozens of businesses and homes were also destroyed.

*In October 1947, fires devastated huge areas of Maine, including Bar Harbor and Acadia National Park. On Mount Desert Island, more than 17,000 acres were destroyed by fire, including more than 10,000 acres of parkland. Also destroyed were 67 summer cottages, 5 grand hotels, and 170 year-round homes. Property damage exceeded $23 million.*

**Q. BY WHAT NAME WAS BANGOR SUPPOSED TO BE CALLED?**

A. Sunbury. According to legend, settlers sent Reverend Seth Noble to Boston to name their town Sunbury, but for some reason he changed his mind along the way and named it Bangor, after his favorite Irish hymn. He and his fellow towns-people were obviously not singing from the same hymnal.

**Q. WHAT BRITISH CAPTAIN IN 1775 LED A NEARLY TWELVE-HOUR BOM-BARDMENT OF FALMOUTH (PORTLAND) THAT NEARLY DESTROYED THE CITY?**

A. Captain Henry Mowat of the Royal Navy. He pounded Portland with sixty-four guns, destroying much of the city, including its library, town hall, and Anglican Church.

**Q. IN WHAT YEAR WAS THE "KING'S HIGHWAY" FROM KITTERY TO PORTLAND BUILT?**

A. 1653. That road formed the basis for what would eventually become U.S. Route 1.

## Q. WHEN WERE THE FIRST RAILROAD TRACKS COMPLETED IN MAINE?

A. 1836. The tracks were completed by the Bangor and Piscataquis Canal and Railroad, and ran from Bangor to Old Town. This was the second railroad built in New England.

## Q. IN WHAT YEAR DID THE FIRST PASSENGER TRAIN BEGIN SERVICE IN MAINE?

A. 1842.

*This reminds me of a story about old Carlton Rich, who loved to travel by train.*

*Carlton was sitting in his seat when the conductor came by, stopped beside Carlton's seat, and said, "Can't leave your bag in the aisle; it's got to be stowed above!" The conductor then stepped lively toward the back of the train.*

*As was his custom, Carlton said nothing. He just sat quietly in his seat, looking out the window.*

*Fifteen minutes later the same fast-moving conductor was back. Again, he stopped beside Carlton's seat and snapped, "I said you can't leave your bag in the aisle. You've got to stow it above."*

*Again, Carlton said nothing. He just sat there in his seat, looking out the window, as the conductor moved quickly toward the front of the train.*

*Like clockwork the conductor was back in another fifteen minutes. But this time, when he stopped at Carlton's seat, he didn't say a word. All in a huff, the conductor reached down with both hands, grabbed the offending bag, walked to the door of the train, opened it, and heaved the bag out into the puckerbrush.*

*Passengers on that side of the train, including Carlton, watched as the bag broke open and its contents were soon spread for fifty yards along the tracks.*

*The conductor walked casually back to Carlton's seat and said, "There! What do you think of that?"*

*Carlton looked at the conductor, then turned and glanced out the window and said, quietly, "I probably wouldn't think much of it—if it were my bag."*

**Q. WHEN WAS MAINE'S FIRST LOTTERY ESTABLISHED?**

A. Maine's first lottery was authorized by the Maine Legislature in 1832 to help raise $50,000 for the Cumberland and Oxford Canal that would connect the largest lakes west of Portland with the seaport. The Canal Bank of Portland was chartered in 1825 to finance the project.

**Q. WHAT WAS THE CONNECTION BETWEEN JOHN HANCOCK—THE FAMOUS SIGNER OF THE DECLARATION OF INDEPENDENCE—AND YORK VILLAGE?**

A. He owned Hancock Wharf, a failed enterprise in the village.

**Q. WHERE AND WHEN WAS MAINE'S FIRST LOBSTER POUND LOCATED?**

A. Vinalhaven Island, in 1875.

**Q. MAINE HAS MORE THAN SIXTY LIGHTHOUSES ALONG ITS COAST AND ISLANDS. THE FIRST LIGHTHOUSE COMMISSIONED BY THE FEDERAL GOVERNMENT WAS PORTLAND HEAD LIGHT. WHICH U.S. PRESIDENT COMMISSIONED THE FAMED LIGHTHOUSE?**

A. George Washington.

**Q. WHERE IN MAINE WILL YOU FIND THE OLDEST SURVIVING PUBLIC BUILDING IN THE UNITED STATES?**

A. York. The Old Gaol was built in 1719 and operated until 1879. It is now a museum and National Historic Landmark.

**Q. WHAT KENNEBUNKPORT ATTRACTION BILLS ITSELF AS THE WORLD'S OLDEST AND LARGEST MUSEUM OF ITS TYPE?**

A. The Seashore Trolley Museum on Log Cabin Road. The key words are "of its type."

**Q. WHO BUILT PORTLAND'S WADSWORTH LONGFELLOW HOUSE?**

A. General Peleg Wadsworth, Henry Wadsworth Longfellow's maternal grandfather.

**Q. IN 1775, THE FIRST NAVAL BATTLE OF THE REVOLUTIONARY WAR WAS FOUGHT OFF THE COAST NEAR THIS DOWN EAST TOWN.**

A. Machias. On June 12, in what some call "The Lexington of the Seas," locals led by Benjamin Foster and Jeremiah O'Brien captured the British ship *Margaretta*, the first prize of the war. The *Margaretta* was refitted as a privateer. The ship's captain was fatally wounded during the battle while the crew was transferred to a prison near Boston.

**Q. ON WHAT MAINE RIVER DID THE AMERICANS SUFFER A NAVAL DEFEAT SO DEVASTATING THAT IT WOULD STAND AS THE NATION'S WORST NAVAL DISASTER UNTIL PEARL HARBOR?**

A. The Penobscot River. The Penobscot Expedition was the largest American naval expedition of the American Revolutionary War. In 1779, British forces began establishing a fortification in what is now Castine. That July, an American force, which boasted 19 armed ships mounting 344 guns and 24 transports, and more than 1,200 men, began attacking the British. However, the Americans were ultra-cautious and essentially lay siege by not pressing the attack.

In mid-August, the Royal Navy reinforcements arrived. The American fleet initially massed to fight, but then turned and fled up the Penobscot River, where they were pinned. The entire American fleet was either sunk by the British or scuttled by the Americans themselves. The men fled into the woods. Those who survived traveled through dense wilderness back to Boston. Overall, the Americans lost 43 ships and approximately 500 men.

**Q. AMERICA'S FIRST CHARTERED CITY WAS LOCATED IN MAINE. CAN YOU NAME IT?**

A. York, in 1641. Indeed, it wasn't New York; it wasn't Philadelphia, or even Duluth.

**Q. WHERE WAS AMERICA'S FIRST VETERANS HOSPITAL LOCATED?**

A. Togus. It was founded in 1866 and located just outside of Augusta.

**Q. AMERICA'S FIRST SAWMILL WAS ESTABLISHED IN 1623 NEAR WHAT MAINE CITY?**

A. York. Yes, York again! America's first sawmill was established near York in 1623.

**Q. WHAT WAS THE FIRST TOWN INCORPORATED IN MAINE?**

A. Kittery, in 1647.

**Q. IN 1794, THIS BECAME MAINE'S FIRST COLLEGE.**

A. Bowdoin College in Brunswick. The college was chartered in 1794, and classes commenced in 1802. The charter was signed by Governor Samuel Adams.

**Q. FOR WHOM IS BOWDOIN COLLEGE NAMED?**

A. Former Massachusetts governor James Bowdoin II.

**Q. WHO OR WHAT WERE *LUTHER LITTLE* AND *HESPER*?**

A. They were the names of the two four-masted schooners that sat, rotting, for years on the banks of the Sheepscot River in the town of Wiscasset, eventually becoming a tourist attraction.

Some say the folks of Wiscasset let them rot instead of trying to preserve them because both vessels were built in Massachusetts, which sounds plausible. They were only supposed to stay there until the shipping business got better, but then the Great Depression began, and by the time things got better the ships were beyond repair. Boat owners have been afraid to beach their vessels on the Sheepscot ever since.

**Q. TRUE OR FALSE: IN THE 1830S, THE STATE OF MAINE SENT 10,000 TROOPS INTO THE AROOSTOOK VALLEY REGION IN ANTICIPATION OF WAR WITH OUR NEIGHBORS IN CANADA.**

A. True. The conflict was known as the Aroostook War.

Now, the Aroostook War was an undeclared and bloodless war that almost flared up because England and the United States couldn't agree on exactly where the border was between our country and the province of New Brunswick. Since way back, the Brits had claimed all the land above Mars Hill. I can hear the cynical "Northern Massachusetts" readers among you saying, "And we were prepared to fight and die for whatever's above Mars Hill?" In a word, yes. We had just about had it with the British by this time, so in January of 1839, a land agent named Rufus McIntire took a posse into the disputed area and started arresting lumberjacks who were cutting down trees on disputed land. Not surprisingly, Rufus was eventually arrested by Canadian officials, and then Mainers started getting a tad annoyed. Within two months there were 10,000

Maine troops either encamped along the Aroostook River or marching toward the spot.

In Washington, the federal government authorized a force of 50,000 men and a budget of $10 million in the event of war. That's how much we cared about the land above Mars Hill. Anyway, the Brits—convinced that they'd stirred up a hornet's nest—decided to talk peace, and after a few sessions of haggling and dickering, they eventually signed the Webster-Ashburton Treaty in 1842, which set the line between us once and for all.

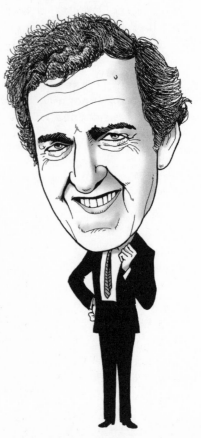

**Q. WHEN THIS MAN WAS ELECTED GOVERNOR IN 1954, HE WAS THE FIRST DEMOCRAT TO HOLD THE POSITION IN TWO DECADES, AND WHEN HE WAS ELECTED MAINE'S U.S. SENATOR IN 1958, HE WAS THE FIRST DEMOCRAT TO HOLD THAT POSITION IN FOUR DECADES. WHO WAS HE?**

A. Edmund S. Muskie (1914–1996) of Rumford.

**Q: WHAT DOES THE "S" IN EDMUND S. MUSKIE STAND FOR?**

A: Sixtus.

Ask some people and they'll tell you that Maine now has a strong two-party political system. Ask other people the same question and they'll say Maine has no organized political parties—just Democrats and Republicans. It's also rumored that there's something called the Green Party in Maine, but I think it's essentially just a couple of kids laid off from the coffeehouse, looking for seasonal work.

It hasn't always been like this. Even after Muskie came on the scene, Maine remained one of the most Republican states in the nation. Back then, folks in the Down East town of Cherryfield would hold an election and then go down to the town hall to count up the ballots. The total would always be: Republicans, 293 votes; Democrats, 0.

I remember back when Democrat John F. Kennedy ran for president against Richard Nixon. I wasn't old enough to vote, but I followed the day-to-day campaign closely. On election night I went down to the town hall to watch the ballot counting, and as they went through the pile it was one Republican vote after another.

Then, about halfway through the pile, they came across a ballot marked "Kennedy." The smoothly running process came to a screeching halt as a poll official fished out the unusual ballot and passed it around the table for all to examine.

"Where'd that come from?" asked First Selectman Arthur Strout.

"I don't know," said clearly annoyed Third Selectman Sherm Ames.

As the curious ballot went around the table, almost everyone had a snide comment about who may have cast the vote, but in the end they begrudgingly concluded that the ballot looked legal and therefore probably had to be counted.

Continuing the count, all the remaining ballots were landing in the Republican pile, until they came to the second-to-last one, and darned if it wasn't another marked "Kennedy."

Well, that's all Second Selectman Ed Beal could stand. He jumped to his feet, grabbed the offending ballot, and said: "The son of a bitch must have voted twice!"

So, they ripped up both errant ballots and the final vote—as usual—was Republicans, 293, Democrats, 0.

**Q. WHAT IS ANOTHER NAME FOR PORTLAND'S FAMED VICTORIA MANSION?**

A. The Morse-Libby House.

**Q. WHAT MAKES THE SCHOONER *STEPHEN TABER* SPECIAL?**

A. The schooner, built in 1871, is the oldest documented sailing vessel in continuous service in the United States. It is designated a National Historic Landmark. It is also part of the windjammer fleet that sails each week in the summer out of Rockland.

**Q. IN WHAT YEAR DID THE LAST RIVER LOG DRIVE TAKE PLACE IN MAINE, AND ON WHAT RIVER?**

A. 1976, on the Kennebec River. Environmental concerns and changing technology brought an end to the log drives, closing out a remarkable era in Maine history.

**Q: WHICH MAINE GOVERNOR HAD THE SHORTEST TIME IN OFFICE?**

A: Nathaniel Haskell, who served for just twenty-five hours in 1953.

**Q. IN 1953, WHAT STATION BECAME MAINE'S FIRST TELEVISION STATION?**

A. WABI-TV of Bangor.

**Q. WHEN DID MAINE PASS THE ADULT SEAT-BELT LAW?**

A. 1995.

*I remember I was up to the country store in Greenville shortly after the seat-belt law was passed, just having coffee with a contingent of local scholars, commentators, and observers. Charlie Farron, the local sheriff's deputy, eventually walked in to join us.*

*Now, I don't know what kind of work you do, but I know there are few jobs tougher these days than the job of enforcing the law throughout this land.*

*When he took on his policing job twenty-six years ago, Charlie thought he was just getting into law enforcement—meaning, he thought he'd be doing just police work (and, of course, waiting for that good pension). But these days, Charlie says the police also have to act as marriage counselors, babysitters, substance abuse experts, and public relations officials.*

*One reason I like Charlie Farron is because he's always got a good story. The other day, Charlie told me about the fella he stopped recently for having a headlight out. As Charlie approached the car, he noticed the fella wasn't wearing his seat belt.*

*When Charlie reminded the fella that Maine law now required the wearing of seat belts, the man got all in a huff and said, "Officer, I know all about the seat-belt law, thank you very much, and I had my belt on. I just now unbuckled it to get my driver's license."*

*Well, Charlie didn't know what to do but ask the fella's wife, who, according to Charlie, looked like an honest Maine woman.*

*"Ma'am," said Charlie, "I'll let you settle this for us here. As far as you know, was your husband wearing his seat belt, or not?"*

*The wife said, "Officer, I've been married to Barney here a long time. And if there's one thing I've learned in all those years, it's to never argue with him when he's been drinking."*

**Q. WHO WAS THE FIRST WOMAN TO HAVE HER NAME PLACED INTO NOMINATION FOR PRESIDENT BY A MAJOR POLITICAL PARTY?**

A. Senator Margaret Chase Smith (1897–1995). When asked by a reporter what she would do if she woke up one morning and found herself in the White House, Senator Smith's classic "Maine" answer was: "I'd apologize to Mrs. Eisenhower and go home." In her remarkable career, Smith was also the first woman to serve in both houses of Congress, and the first woman to represent Maine in either. She is perhaps best known for her 1950 speech, "Declaration of Conscience," in which she criticized the tactics of

Senator Joseph McCarthy. She served as a U.S. representative from 1940 to 1949, and as a U.S. senator from 1949 to 1973.

### Q. WHAT FORMER PRESIDENT STILL HAS A SUMMER HOME IN MAINE?

A. George H. W. Bush, America's forty-first president, has a summer home on Walker's Point in the coastal town of Kennebunkport.

### Q. WHO WAS CAPTAIN SAMUEL ARGALL?

A. In the struggle between England and France for control of North America, Captain Argall drew first blood on Mount Desert Island in 1613 when he destroyed a French post. Tourists were unaffected because they thought it was just a local dinner theater doing improv.

### Q. WHO WAS CAPTAIN CHARLES D. SIGSBEE?

A. Commander of the battleship *Maine*, which sank in Havana Harbor on February 15, 1898. The United States declared war against Spain a few months later, on April 25.

# NATURE AND WILDLIFE

**Q. ELSEWHERE THESE PESKY INSECTS ARE SOMETIMES CALLED "BUF-FALO GNATS" OR "TURKEY GNATS." WHAT ARE THEY CALLED IN MAINE?**

A. Blackflies. Being a wholesome, family-oriented book, we won't include many of the earthy nouns, verbs, and participles used to describe the blackfly and the black-fly "experience." We're told that blackflies may have been first introduced into Maine as part of a govern-ment-sponsored pro-gram to help curb the burgeoning tourist population. However, not only do we now have more blackflies (and tourists) than ever before, but they also

49

arrive earlier and leave later each year. Typical government program.

**Q. WE DON'T MEAN TO "BUG" YOU, BUT HOW MANY SPECIES OF INSECTS MAKE THEIR HOME IN MAINE? GO AHEAD, TAKE A GUESS.**

A. I don't blame you if you guessed "two"—the blackfly and the mosquito—but you're way off. On the other hand, if you've ever been camping in Maine and forgot the bug spray, you probably know that more than 16,000 distinct insect species make their home in Maine. We just hope their home isn't your home.

**Q. WHERE CAN YOU GO TO SEE THE SUN RISE BEFORE ANYONE ELSE IN THE COUNTRY?**

A. In winter, the top of Cadillac Mountain is the first to see the sun. Folks in the Aroostook County town of Mars Hill claim they see the sun first from mid-March to mid-September. And folks in Lubec say that right in between, at the spring and fall equinoxes, you can see the sun first at West Quoddy Head, the peninsula that is the easternmost part of Maine. Most people don't really care who sees the sun first as long as it comes up.

**Q. HOW MANY YEARS HAS IT BEEN SINCE A RATTLESNAKE WAS SEEN IN MAINE?**

A. Unless you've snuck one by us in your luggage recently, it's been more than 100 years since a rattler has been seen in Maine. And they haven't been missed. We just hope the number of years of their absence keeps getting higher and higher.

**Q. WHAT MAINE SEABIRD IS KNOWN AS A "SEA PARROT"?**

A. The Atlantic puffin.

**Q. HOW MANY COYOTES ARE THERE IN MAINE?**

A. We haven't counted them ourselves, and no one has done a one-by-one nose count, but experts say there are between 10,000 and 16,000. I know that's quite a spread, but it's the best answer we have. You could always try to count them yourself, but it'll probably take a while. If you're a tourist, why not take a few coyotes home with you when you leave? We won't miss them.

**Q. HOW MANY SPECIES OF WHALES AND PORPOISES HAVE BEEN SPOTTED OFF THE MAINE COAST?**

A. Like we've said before, we haven't counted them ourselves, but we're told by those who claim they have that more than twenty species of whales, dolphins, and porpoises have been spotted.

**Q. ALTHOUGH SOME ADULT MALES CAN GROW TO WEIGH AS MUCH AS 600 POUNDS, HOW MUCH DOES A TYPICAL NEWBORN BEAR CUB WEIGH?**

A. About twelve ounces.

**Q. HOW MUCH COULD THAT SAME BEAR CUB WEIGH AT THE END OF ITS
FIRST SUMMER?**

A. About seventy-five pounds. And that's mostly from a diet of
Maine blueberries, so if you're watching your weight, be care-
ful with those blueberries. (Just kidding!)

*Speaking of bears, I love a good bear story. I once asked my old uncle Perley if he'd ever run into any bears in all his years in Maine. Of course, he had. He said, "I was out picking blueberries on a hot day when I came to the end of a patch and looked up, and there, staring me dead in the eye, was a three-hundred-pound black bear, just sitting there picking his own berries."*

*"What did you do, Uncle?" I asked.*

*"I dropped my berries and got up and ran."*

*"What'd the bear do?"*

*"He dropped his berries and got up and chased me. And the more I ran, the more he chased me. I'd scamper up a tree and he, of course, would scamper right up behind me. I'd climb down the other side and he was right there. Running up steep hills didn't slow him down at all. He kept running right behind me.*

*"Finally, I ran out onto a frozen pond and he was afraid to follow me. Eventually he got tired of waiting and ambled off into the woods."*

*"Wait a minute," I said. "Wait a minute, Uncle Perley, weren't you pickin' blueberries?"*

*"That's right," said Uncle Perley.*

*"But you said you were chased onto a frozen pond."*

*"Ayuh," said Uncle Perley. "That friggin' bear chased me from August all the way to Christmas!"*

**Q. WHAT CAUSES MEDICINE-BALL-SIZE BURLS ON SOME COASTAL SPRUCE TREES?**

A. While some of the burls are caused by a virus, many are caused by sea salt being forced into the bark by winter winds.

**Q. HOW MANY SPECIES OF BIRDS HAVE BEEN SPOTTED IN MAINE?**

A. Even though only about a dozen different species of birds have visited Mother's and my feeders over the years, more than 400 different species have been spotted in Maine. I guess our all-you-can-eat birdseed bar isn't suitable for all birds.

**Q. OTHER THAN THE FACT THAT IT HAS A LOT OF BEAVERS, WHAT IS A KEY REASON THAT MAINE HAS A LOT OF BEAVER DAMS?**

A. Some might say it's because beavers are exempt from the permitting process, which is true, but another reason is the fact that it's against the law to disturb any part of a beaver dam.

**Q. SOME CALL THEM "BUSHY-TAILED RATS," OTHERS CALL THEM CUNNIN'. THE QUESTION IS: HOW MANY GRAY SQUIRRELS ARE THERE IN MAINE?**

A. The best guess is about twenty million.

**Q. HOW DO MAINE CHICKADEES REMEMBER WHERE THEY STORED ALL THEIR SEEDS?**

A. No, they don't write it down; don't be silly. Chickadees just expand their brain capacity as winter gets near. Problem solved. This is in contrast to some of our politicians who, some people claim, shrink their brain capacity once they are elected.

**Q. MAINE HAS NO POISONOUS SNAKES, BUT WE DO HAVE SOME LARGE SNAKES THAT CAN BECOME UNPLEASANT IF CORNERED OR CAPTURED. WHAT IS THE LARGEST SNAKE FOUND IN MAINE?**

A. The black racer, which can grow to be six feet in length. The name "racer" is apt because this snake is very fast and will flee from danger. If cornered it can get downright ugly, and will bite. It can also rattle its tail in dry leaves and do a pretty good impersonation of a rattlesnake. If you capture one, be prepared for it to writhe, defecate on you, and spray musk all over you. Or, you could just leave it alone.

**Q. THIS PEATLAND, WHICH MEASURES ROUGHLY 7,000 ACRES, IS CALLED MAINE'S GREAT HEATH. WHERE IS IT LOCATED?**

A. Down East, with the southern portion located in the town of Columbia. That's one big bog.

**Q. WHAT IS CONSIDERED THE LARGEST MEMBER OF THE DEER FAMILY?**

A. Moose. A mature male can weigh up to 1,500 pounds, which would be considered large in any family, and is why the moose shops in the Deer Big & Tall shops, when it shops.

**Q. WHAT DOES THE ABENAKI WORD MUSQUASH REFER TO?**

A. Musquash is the Abenaki word for muskrat. The muskrat's name in our language comes from two scent glands near its tail that give off a strong "musky" odor, which the muskrat uses to mark its territory. Aren't you glad we humans have advanced to things like surveyor's stakes to mark our territories?

**Q. HOW DOES THE SNOWSHOE HARE CAMOUFLAGE ITSELF?**

A. Its fur turns snow-white in winter and rusty-brown in summer and fall.

**Q. LET'S SLOW THINGS DOWN HERE WITH A QUESTION ABOUT TURTLES. WHAT THREE SPECIES OF MARINE TURTLES ARE FOUND IN THE GULF OF MAINE?**

A. Leatherback, loggerhead, and Kemp's ridley (also called Atlantic ridley). The leatherback and loggerhead are some of the largest marine turtles; the Kemp's ridley is one of the smallest of marine turtles. All three are endangered species, so just leave them alone, okay?

**Q. SPEAKING OF THE GULF OF MAINE, WHAT ARE ITS EASTERN AND WESTERN BOUNDARIES?**

A. To the west, Nantucket Shoals; to the east, Cape Sable.

**Q. WHAT FOUR SPECIES OF OWLS ARE MOST COMMONLY FOUND THROUGHOUT MAINE?**

A. Barred, great horned, northern saw-whet, and eastern screech. It's hard to say which is the wiser.

**Q. WHAT ORGANIZATION IS WORKING FOR THE RETURN OF THE WOLF TO MAINE?**

A. You're correct in assuming it's not Red Riding Hood's descendants, or Maine's native sheep population. No, it's a group called the Maine Wolf Coalition. We think it was Ben Franklin who said, "Pure democracy is two wolves and a lamb voting on what to have for lunch."

**Q. WHAT PERCENTAGE OF MAINE PEOPLE REPORT THAT THEY HAVE SEEN A MOOSE?**

A. One survey found that 87 percent of Mainers claim to have seen a moose. For the record, I have seen several moose in Maine so far, and even wrote a book with "moose" in the title. Do I get extra points for that?

**Q. WHAT IS MAINE'S BIGGEST TREE?**

A. As of 2011, Maine had three trees on the National Register of Big Trees that were champions in their class. The nation's largest known yellow birch tree is in Wayne, and measures 82 feet high and 242 inches around. We've also got a champion black spruce, in Brooklin, and a champion bigtooth aspen, in Appleton. Each state keeps a Register of Big Trees, and if you see a really big one, you can nominate it.

**Q. HOW MUCH WEIGHT DOES A MAINE RACCOON ADD JUST BEFORE WINTER?**

A. Some raccoons double their weight just before winter. I know some Patriots fans who do the same thing, while sitting, like a plump Kennebec russet, remote in hand, in front of the fifty-two-inch flat-screen TV during football season.

**Q. WHAT SHOULD YOU DO IF YOU MEET A BLACK BEAR IN THE MAINE WOODS?**

A. Experts say you should back away slowly; do not turn and run. And whatever you do, don't give the bear your credit card number or the last four digits of your "social," no matter how persistent he may be.

*That reminds me of yet another bear story. A couple of years ago, this fella from New Jersey came to Maine to see what it was like to spend a week in the Great North Woods.*

*This fella hired himself a Maine guide from down to Grand Lake Stream by answering an ad in a sportsman's magazine. And he got one of the best, my old neighbor, Murray Seavey. Murray picked this fella up at the Bangor International Airport, loaded his fancy, new gear into the truck, and headed to his camp up-country.*

*As they drove along, the New Jersey fella looked out the window at the miles and miles of woods and began to wonder just what it was he was getting himself into. Being born and raised in* the city, he'd never spent much time around trees—at least, not as many as he now saw through the truck window as they sped down the road.

For years he had talked about having what people in the city call "a wilderness experience," or what Mainers call "a trip to camp." And now, here he was.

When they got to camp, Murray got right to work setting things up. By now the New Jersey fella was so nervous about being in the wild woods of Maine that he was afraid to let Murray out of his sight, and followed him around camp like a puppy.

At one point Murray finally turned to him and said, "Look, why don't you make yourself useful and take that bucket down to the spring and get us some water while I finish building us a fire in the stove for supper."

Wanting to be agreeable, the fella took the bucket and went out the door, down the path to the spring. Five minutes later he was back, white as a ghost, the bucket in his hand rattling away.

Murray took one look at him and said, "What in the world is wrong with you?"

The fella from New Jersey said, "Well, I went down to the spring like you asked me, and when I got there I saw what must have been a three-hundred-pound black bear standing right up to his waist in the spring!"

"And that's what's got you all scared to death?" Murray asked, scratching his beard.

"Well, yes," said the New Jersey fella, a little annoyed at Murray's reaction.

"Let me tell you something," said Murray. "I guarantee you, that black bear was as scared of you as you were of him!"

"Is that true?" asked the fella, now a tad embarrassed.

"That is absolutely true," said Murray, emphatically.

"In that case," said the fella, with a little chuckle, "that spring water isn't fit to drink, now, anyway."

The mysterious creature from the briny deep!

SEA HOG

**Q. WHAT DID SOME OF MAINE'S FIRST ENGLISH SETTLERS CALL WHALES?**

A. Sea hogs. We're sure the whales would have called the settlers worse if they could have.

**Q. HOW MANY YEARS HAS THE GREAT BLUE HERON (CONSIDERED THE WORLD'S GREATEST FISHERMAN) BEEN VISITING THE MAINE COAST?**

A. According to fossils found, the blue heron has been visiting the Maine coast for more than forty million years. However, they are not native to the area. They're seasonal visitors, so they're still considered "from away," and even though they're hatched here, their offspring are not considered native either.

**Q. WHAT DO DOWN EAST FAMILIES MAKE WITH TIPS AND BOUGHS?**

A. Christmas wreaths.

**Q. WHAT DO MAINE'S BLACK BEARS PREFER TO EAT IN THE SUMMER?**

A. Wild cherries, blackberries, raspberries, and wild Maine blueberries. You'd think with a diet like that they'd be a little more trim, wouldn't you?

**Q. WHAT IS A WEATHER STICK?**

A. A stick that can tell you when it's going to rain. Yes, I'm serious. Weather sticks are made from balsam fir or birch rods. They point up in low humidity and down in high humidity. Do they work? Well, a good weather stick has as good an average as your average high-paid TV weatherman or woman, and doesn't need computers, satellite feeds, or any of the other digital gizmos modern meteorologists use.

My grandfather had a weather stick, as well as a thermometer, barometer, wind gauge, and tide chart, and he was the most accurate predictor of weather I've ever known. You'd ask him how long the overcast would last and he'd look at his instruments, check his wind gauge, weather stick, and tide chart, and say, "These clouds should be gone by low water," and it seemed they always were.

**Q. TRUE OR FALSE: IN 1816, MAINERS SAW SNOW IN JUNE, AND FROST IN BOTH JULY AND AUGUST.**

A. True. The year is also known as Eighteen Hundred and Froze to Death.

**Q. ON AVERAGE, WHAT IS MAINE'S WARMEST MONTH?**

A. July (77 degrees is the average high in Portland).

AYUH, THAT'S MIGHTY INTERESTING, JOHN!

*The Scarborough Marsh Wildlife Management Area is 3,100 acres. According to the Friends of Scarborough Marsh, the area is owned and managed by Maine's Department of Inland Fisheries and Wildlife, and includes a total of five tidal rivers, several smaller streams, some coastal freshwater marsh, tidal flats, and almost 200 acres of upland habitat.*

**Q. ON AVERAGE, WHAT IS MAINE'S COLDEST MONTH?**

A. January (5 degrees is the average low in Portland; 0 degrees in Caribou).

**Q. HOW MANY MILES OF THE FAMED APPALACHIAN TRAIL ARE IN MAINE? WHAT'S OUR OTHER AT CLAIM TO FAME?**

A. 281 miles. And the trail ends (or starts, depending on how you look at it) atop Maine's highest point, Mount Katahdin.

**Q. TRUE OR FALSE: ONLY FEMALE BLACKFLIES BITE.**

A. True.

**Q. WHAT PERCENTAGE OF MAINE BLUEBERRIES ARE SOLD FRESH?**

A. Less than 1 percent, and a lot of them are eaten by bears.

# WILD CARD QUESTIONS

**Q. THIS PORTLAND NATIVE AND FORMER STATE REPRESENTATIVE, STATE SENATOR, AND GOVERNOR DONATED THE 202,064 ACRES OF LAND NOW KNOWN AS BAXTER STATE PARK TO THE STATE.**

A. Percival Baxter (1876–1969).

**Q. THIS HAMPDEN NATIVE WAS A NURSE AND A PIONEER IN CHANGING THE WAY THE MENTALLY ILL AND HANDICAPPED ARE TREATED IN AMERICA. SHE PETITIONED STATE LEGISLATURES TO ALLOCATE MONEY TO CREATE PROPERLY RUN MENTAL INSTITUTIONS.**

A. Dorothea Dix (1802–1878). Dix traveled to hospitals and prisons across the country and saw firsthand the deplorable manner in which the mentally ill and handicapped were treated, prompting her to take action. In addition, Dix served as the supervisor of nurses for the Union Army during the Civil War.

**Q. WHO IN 1888 BECAME THE ONLY MAINE NATIVE EVER SELECTED AS CHIEF JUSTICE OF THE U.S. SUPREME COURT?**

A. Melville Fuller (1833–1910). Fuller was born in Augusta and educated at Bowdoin College. He presided over the Supreme Court from 1888 until his death in 1910.

**Q. THIS MANCHESTER NATIVE BECAME AN INTERNATIONAL SENSATION AND CAPTURED THE HEARTS OF THE WORLD WHEN SHE WROTE A LETTER TO SOVIET PREMIER YURI ANDROPOV, EXPRESSING HER FEARS ABOUT A POSSIBLE NUCLEAR HOLOCAUST.**

A. Samantha Smith (1972–1985). Following her letter, Andropov invited Smith to visit the Soviet Union, making her one of our nation's youngest peace ambassadors. Smith and her father were killed in a plane crash in 1985.

**Q. MAINE NATIVE AND WESTBROOK HIGH SCHOOL GRADUATE KEVIN EASTMAN CREATED WHAT FAMOUS COMIC BOOK AND ANIMATED CHARACTERS?**

A. The Teenage Mutant Ninja Turtles. In 1984, Eastman and collaborator Peter Laird spent $1,200 to self-publish the first edition of *The Teenage Mutant Ninja Turtles*.

**Q. NAME THE NORTHERNMOST COMMUNITY IN MAINE AND NEW ENGLAND.**

A. Estcourt Station, Maine, a tiny village in Big Twenty Township. While there are logging roads into town, Estcourt Station has no public roads that connect it to Maine. Travelers must travel into Canada, then cross into the village by using a public road.

*E*stcourt Station is located at the southern end of Canada's Lake Pohenegamook. According to legend, a giant sea monster named Ponik inhabits the lake and flips over boats on the lake to eat the passengers.

**Q. JOHN BACON CURTIS WAS AN AMERICAN BUSINESSMAN AND INVENTOR WHOSE PORTLAND COMPANY BECAME THE FIRST TO COMMERCIALLY PRODUCE WHAT PRODUCT?**

A. Chewing gum. Curtis (1827–1897) produced "State of Maine Pure Spruce Gum," starting in 1848. At one point, after Curtis began adding sweeteners and flavors to his gum, the Curtis Company employed more than 200 people in Portland.

**Q. WHAT DOES WABANAKI MEAN IN ENGLISH?**

A. People of the Dawn.

**Q. NAME THE FOUR WABANAKI TRIBES LOCATED IN MAINE.**

A. Penobscot, Passamaquoddy, Micmac, and Maliseet.

**Q. THE FIRST NATIONAL PARK EAST OF THE MISSISSIPPI AND THE SECOND-MOST-VISITED NATIONAL PARK IN THE UNITED STATES IS LOCATED IN MAINE. CAN YOU NAME IT?**

A. Acadia National Park on Mount Desert Island.

**Q. WHAT FIRM DESIGNED THE PORTLAND MUSEUM OF ART?**

A. I. M. Pei & Associates, in 1983.

AYUH, THAT'S MIGHTY INTERESTING, JOHN!

*In the late 1800s, two Massachusetts men claimed to have developed a method of extracting gold from seawater. In 1897, the two men, Reverend Prescott Jernegan and Charles Fisher, bought an old gristmill in Lubec which they converted into the Electrolytic Marine Salts Company. The two men claimed that millions of dollars (as much as $100 million) were flowing through the Lubec Narrows every day, and that by using special "accumulators," which they had invented, gold could be extracted from seawater. Hundreds of thousands of shares in the company were sold for one dollar each, dozens of workers were hired, and operations began. The first factory was going so well, they made plans to build a second factory and employ hundreds of people. However, in 1898, the two men mysteriously vanished from town, leaving bewildered townspeople and defrauded investors behind. According to some reports, Reverend Jernegan traveled to France under an assumed name and later returned a small portion of the money to his investors.*

**Q. THE LOSS OF THIS PASSENGER STEAMER, WITH ITS APPROXIMATELY 190 PASSENGERS AND CREW, IS WIDELY CONSIDERED THE WORST MARITIME DISASTER IN NEW ENGLAND HISTORY.**

A. The *Portland*. The *Portland* went down in November of 1898 during the Portland Gale, while making its regular run from Portland to Boston.

**Q. IN THE 1930S, THE WORLD'S LARGEST YACHT WAS BUILT AT BATH IRON WORKS FOR J. P. MORGAN. CAN YOU NAME IT?**

A. *Corsair IV*, which means "pirate" or "pirate ship." The *Corsair IV* was the largest yacht built in the United States. If you have to ask how much it cost you obviously couldn't have afforded it, but as long as you asked, the *Corsair IV* is said to have cost J. P. Morgan $2.5 million. And those, of course, were 1930s Depression-era dollars.

**Q. SPEAKING OF EXPENSIVE, THE YACHT *RANGER* WAS ALSO BUILT IN MAINE. CAN YOU TELL ME FOR WHOM IT WAS BUILT, AND ITS CLAIM TO FAME?**

A. *Ranger* was built at Bath Iron Works for Harold S. Vanderbilt, great-grandson of Cornelius Vanderbilt. *Ranger* went on to win the 1937 America's Cup, beating challenger *Endeavour II* from England. After winning the cup, *Ranger* was hauled out and never raced again. It was sold for scrap in 1941, for $12,000.

**Q. WHO FOUNDED MAINE'S BATH IRON WORKS?**

A. Thomas W. Hyde, who was also a Civil War general and Medal of Honor recipient.

**Q. WHAT SHOULD YOU THINK OF WHEN YOU HEAR THE WORDS RED JACKET?**

A. Don't think haberdasher or fancy restaurant; think ship-yard. *Red Jacket* was a clipper ship built at the George Thomas shipyard in Thomaston in 1854, and considered the fastest sailing ship in the world. She holds the transatlantic record for sailing ships, having sailed from New York to Liverpool—dock to dock—in thirteen days, one hour, and twenty-five minutes. She could have made better time if not for the clunky timepieces they had in those days. They couldn't take a licking and keep on ticking.

**Q. IN 1949, HORACE A. HILDRETH FOUNDED THE COMPANY THAT EVENTUALLY LED TO WHAT MAINE FIRST?**

A. Hildreth founded Community Broadcasting Services, which in 1953 put WABI-TV, Maine's first television station, on the air. Gardiner native Hildreth was elected in a landslide to be Maine's fifty-ninth governor, in 1945. Two years later, he was reelected for a second term by another wide margin.

**Q. IN 1862, HENRY FRANKLIN MORTON FOUNDED THE PARIS MANUFACTURING COMPANY IN SOUTH PARIS AND BECAME THE FIRST LARGE-SCALE MAKER OF WHAT PRODUCT?**

A. Sporting sleds. A sled made by Morton's company was used by Arctic explorer Donald MacMillan. Morton's firm grew to become the largest and longest-running sled manufacturer in the country's history.

**Q. WHAT NATIONALLY FAMOUS PRODUCT DID UNION NATIVE DR. AUGUSTIN THOMPSON INVENT?**

A. Moxie. Thompson changed the tonic first known as "impregnated water" to the beverage called "Moxie—Nerve Food." From 1900 to the 1920s, Moxie was America's most popular soft drink. Today, there is still an annual Moxie Festival in Lisbon Falls that takes place every July to celebrate the famous drink.

**Q. What important tool—essential to all year-round Mainers—was invented by Don A. Sargent of Bangor?**

A. The snowplow.

**Q. Speaking of things important in winter, what device was invented by John Alby Spencer of Island Falls?**

A. The thermostat.

**Q. And another winter item (after all, necessity is the mother of invention): What did Chester Greenwood, from Farmington, invent?**

A. Earmuffs.

**Q. Who invented the Stanley Steamer?**

A. Francis E. and Freelan O. Stanley.

**Q. Well, that's fine, but what was the Stanley Steamer?**

A. When they hear it was invented in Maine, some think the Stanley Steamer must have been designed to cook clams, mussels, crabs, and lobsters—or even red hot dogs. That, however, is wrong.

Not to be confused with a Stanley Steemer (that'll clean your carpets), the Stanley Steamer was a lightweight transport vehicle powered by a steam engine that was wicked fast. The Steamer broke all kinds of speed records, some of which still stand today.

Francis and Freelan were identical twins, born in 1849 in Kingfield. They were inventors, artists, violin makers, and all-around creative thinkers. They decided to try to build an automobile powered by steam, and built their first one, more or less from scratch, in 1897. Their company, the Stanley Motor Carriage Company, produced successful steam automobiles well into the 1920s.

The brothers also invented a procedure to develop photographs called a dry-plate process. They manufactured the equipment and eventually sold the Dry Plate Company (with headquarters in Lewiston) to George Eastman of Eastman Kodak.

Freelan, suffering from tuberculosis, moved to Estes Park, Colorado, where he built the now-famous Stanley Hotel in 1909. This hotel, listed on the National Register of Historic Places, is where Stephen King is said to have started writing *The Shining*.

*Milton Bradley, who is credited with starting the board-game industry in America when he created The Checkered Game of Life (eventually, The Game of Life) in 1860, was born in Vienna, Maine.*

**Q. WHO WAS CHARLES FORSTER?**

A. Charles Forster, of Strong, Maine, was the first to mass-produce and market what is probably the world's simplest and least-complicated device—the toothpick. No one has been able to create the digital version of the toothpick; it remains

in its original analog form. Forster came in contact with tooth-picks in South America, while he was a merchant seaman. He eventually started making them to sell when he quit the sea. His toothpick plant was in business from 1860 until it closed in 2002.

**Q. WHO INVENTED THE HOLE IN THE DOUGHNUT?**

A. There's a story going around that in 1847, Elizabeth Gregory, a New England ship captain's mother, made deep-fried dough that used her son's spice cargo of nutmeg, cinnamon, and lemon rind. Because the center of the dough often failed to cook through, clever bakers in those days put apples, raisins, or prunes in the center. Elizabeth made the deep-fried cakes with hazelnuts or walnuts in the middle—hence the term "dough-nuts."

Son Hanson always took credit for putting the hole in the doughnut. Some doughnut historians think that Hanson was a bit of a cheapskate and was just trying to save on food costs. Others say that he gave the doughnut its first hole when, in the middle of a terrible storm, in order to keep both hands on the ship's wheel, he crammed one of his mother's fried sensations onto one of the wooden spokes of the wheel. Still others say he just didn't care for the nuts and pushed them out. He claimed cutting the hole in the center was his idea, and he brought it back to show his mom. Either way, cooks found that the pastries cooked better and more evenly with the hole. And the rest is, well, up to you to decide.

Today, the town of Clam Cove, Maine has a plaque in honor of Captain Hanson Gregory, the man who claims to have invented the hole in the doughnut.

**Q. WHAT SEAL HARBOR SUMMER RESIDENT BUILT THE SPRAWLING 100-ROOM "COTTAGE" NAMED EYRIE IN 1912?**

A. John D. Rockefeller. The Rockefeller family summered at the house on Mount Desert Island for decades, until the family demolished it in 1962.

**Q. WHO IS PAMOLA?**

A. According to Abenaki mythology, Pamola is the protector of Mount Katahdin. He has the head of a moose, the body of a man, and the wings and claws of an eagle. Yes, it does sound like he was designed by a committee or a board of selectmen.

*The First Radio Parish Church of America, established in 1926, is America's oldest continuous religious broadcast. It first aired on WCSH-AM Radio in Portland, originating from the Eastland Hotel.*

## Q. TECHNICALLY, HEALTH CARE IS MAINE'S LARGEST INDUSTRY. CAN YOU NAME THE STATE'S SECOND-LARGEST INDUSTRY?

A. Tourism, of course.

*From Memorial Day to Labor Day, according to the state tourism department, the tourist is supposed to be the most important person in our state—regardless of whether they use cash, check, major credit card, barter, or even text messages. I know what you're thinking—"Does that include the tourists in those enormous, lumbering, slow-moving, gas-guzzling motor homes? Those 100-foot-long, hazardous habitats on wheels?"*

*Well, darn right it does. The folks in the tourism industry have a saying: "A tourist is not an interruption of our lives here in Maine; tourists are the reason we're still alive after our long winters." I've got to admit, even I've been newly educated to the importance of what we used to call "summer complaints" (or worse) back in the day. Now I stand 100 percent behind the state-mandated spirit of actually helping tourists rather than toying with them for our own amusement.*

*Not that I was alone.*

Maine's reputation was so bad, the tourist folks down in Augusta spent, like, a gazillion dollars on a campaign—complete with cunnin' little pamphlets—telling natives how to help summer visitors to make their stay more pleasant.

Was all this necessary? Probably, but by my reckoning, our alleged ignorance of how to treat tourists didn't exactly stop 'em at the border, or even slow 'em down, for that matter. So many people poured into our beautiful state searching for moose, lobsters, and lighthouses that in some areas, tourists outnumbered blackflies and mosquitoes—combined. (In my pre-enlightened days, I might have added that they were just as annoying, too!)

Even if a Mainer forgets the exact how-to-be-polite details, all they really need to know is that from Memorial Day to Labor Day, a tourist—at least, those with money to spend (the rest can just keep on truckin' to Canada)—is the Most Important Person in the State.

Now I agree wholeheartedly with this idea, and want to do my share. So let me just help explain a little about what to do and what not to do when approached by a flatlander.

If faced with the choice of:
  a) directing an elderly woman to an emergency room for life-
       saving treatment, or
  b) personally driving a tourist to the nearest clam shack for
       emergency fried clams and a Coke,
you should, without a moment's hesitation, head for the clam shack.

Here's another example of what not to do:
  "What's the quickest way to Bangor?"
  "Are you going by car?"
  "Yes."
  "Well, that's the quickest way."

Likewise, you should avoid this impolite exchange:

"Excuse me, sir. I'm on my way to Ellsworth; does it make any difference which way I go at this fork in the road?"

"Not to me it don't."

And finally, this is also bad manners:

"Excuse me, sir. Where does this road go?"

"Nowhere. It mostly just sets right here."

Sure, I make fun, but it's an economic fact that with the worming, clear-cutting, and garden ornament industries all struggling, tourism really is important. So I can't blame the state's tourism people for taking the summer-complaint business seriously. Heck, some of them tourism people even go to college for a hospitality degree. I hear they study four long years learning how to make change, how to show people to Room 221, and how to say, "Do you want fries with that?"

**Q. WHAT MAINE GOVERNOR OVERSAW THE IMPLEMENTATION OF THE FIRST INCOME TAX IN MAINE, AND IN WHAT YEAR WAS IT ENACTED?**

A. Governor Kenneth M. Curtis, in 1969.

*F*ormer Maine governor John E. Baldacci is a first cousin once removed of former Maine senator and majority leader George J. Mitchell, and a second cousin of author David Baldacci.

**Q. What U.S. vice president, although never a Maine resident, was born in Bar Harbor on July 8, 1908?**

A. Nelson Aldrich Rockefeller, who was governor of New York (1958–1973) and U.S. vice president under Gerald R. Ford. He was a summer resident of Seal Harbor on Mount Desert Island.

**Q. Finish this famous slogan: "I should have bought it, when I..."?**

A. "... saw it at Marden's." Harold "Micky" Marden built a Maine retailing icon after opening his first store in Fairfield, in 1964.

**Q. How is a Maine frappe different from a milk shake?**

A. A frappe has ice cream in it; a milk shake does not.

*E*very October, the Sunday River Ski Resort in Newry hosts the North American Wife-Carrying Championships. Male contestants must traverse a 278-yard obstacle course while carrying a woman. In 2011, the winners received the woman's weight in beer and five times her weight in cash.

**Q. IN 2009, LINDA BEAN TEAMED WITH AMATO'S TO CREATE THE WORLD'S LONGEST WHAT, AT SIXTY-ONE FEET AND NINE AND A HALF INCHES?**

A. Lobster roll. It contained forty-five pounds of lobster meat.

# SPORTS

**Q. WHAT CHEVERUS HIGH SCHOOL GRADUATE HAS WON FIVE OLYMPIC MEDALS IN SWIMMING—THREE GOLD, ONE SILVER, AND ONE BRONZE?**

A. Ian Crocker. Crocker, who was born in 1982, has competed in three Olympic games—the 2000, 2004, and 2008.

**Q. IAN CROCKER WAS THE FIRST SWIMMER TO BREAK FIFTY-ONE SECONDS IN WHAT SWIMMING EVENT?**

A. The 100-meter butterfly.

**Q. WHAT HAMPDEN ACADEMY GRADUATE, WHO WAS NAMED TO THE 2000 AMERICAN LEAGUE ALL-STAR TEAM, REPLACED THE LEGENDARY CAL RIPKEN AS SHORTSTOP (RIPKEN MOVED TO THIRD BASE) FOR THE BALTIMORE ORIOLES IN 1997?**

A. Mike Bordick. Bordick played for four major league teams from 1990 to 2003, amassing 1,500 hits and compiling a .260 career batting average. He played in one World Series for the New York Mets.

**Q. THE UNIVERSITY OF MAINE WON THE NATIONAL CHAMPIONSHIP IN 1993 AND 1999 IN WHAT SPORT?**

A. Hockey.

**Q. WHO COACHED MAINE'S TWO NATIONAL-CHAMPIONSHIP HOCKEY TEAMS?**

A. Shawn Walsh (1955–2001). Walsh died after a battle with cancer, in September 2001.

**Q. THE UNIVERSITY OF MAINE HOCKEY TEAM PLAYS ITS HOME GAMES IN THE ALFOND ARENA. FOR WHOM IS THE ARENA NAMED?**

A. Harold Alfond (1914–2007). Alfond founded the Dexter Shoe Company and established the first factory outlet store. Alfond and his family, through the Harold Alfond Foundation, have donated tens of millions of dollars to charitable causes, helping to build several college athletic stadiums and fields.

**Q. WHAT GRADUATE OF SOUTH PORTLAND HIGH SCHOOL AND THE UNIVERSITY OF MAINE LED THE NATIONAL LEAGUE IN EARNED RUN AVERAGE WHILE PITCHING FOR THE SAN FRANCISCO GIANTS IN 1992?**

A. Billy Swift. Swift, who won a silver medal while pitching for the U.S. in the 1984 Olympics, also won twenty-one games that year. For his major league career, he was 94–78, with a 3.95 ERA.

**Q. CAPE ELIZABETH–BORN JOAN BENOIT WAS THE FIRST WOMAN TO EVER WIN WHAT SPORTING EVENT?**

A. The women's Olympic marathon. She won the gold medal at the 1984 Summer Olympics in Los Angeles, the year that the women's marathon was introduced.

**Q. WHILE HER CLAIM TO FAME WAS AS AN OLYMPIC MARATHON CHAMPION, WHAT SPORT DID JOAN BENOIT FIRST PLAY AT CAPE ELIZABETH HIGH SCHOOL?**

A. Field hockey.

**Q. WHAT MAINE RESIDENT WAS CROWNED THE FIRST OLYMPIC SNOWBOARD CROSS CHAMPION?**

A. Seth Wescott, who lives in Carrabassett Valley, won the inaugural event at the 2006 Winter Olympics in Torino, Italy.

**Q. Who was Bert Roberge?**

A. A University of Maine pitcher who pitched in the major leagues for six years with the Houston Astros, Chicago White Sox, and Montreal Expos, mostly as a reliever. He compiled a 12–12 career record, with a 3.98 ERA.

**Q. Who is the only boxer from Maine to win a world boxing title?**

A. Joey Gamache of Lewiston, who won not just one but two world boxing titles—the WBA Super Featherweight title in 1991, and the WBA Lightweight title in 1991. Just be advised: Don't call Joey a "lightweight."

**Q. In 1965, these two heavyweight boxers fought for the title at St. Dominic's Arena in Lewiston.**

A. On May 25, 1965, Muhammad Ali (then known as Cassius Clay) defeated Sonny Liston in one minute and twelve seconds of the first round.

**Q. What forgetful singer sang a tortured version of the National Anthem at the Clay-Liston heavyweight bout in Lewiston?**

A. Robert ("What's this song, again?") Goulet, who forgot the words.

**Q. Who was known as the "Deerfoot of the Diamond"?**

A. Louis Sockalexis. Sockalexis, a member of the Penobscot tribe, is said to be the first Native American to play in the major leagues.

**Q. WHAT MEMBER OF THE BOSTON RED SOX HALL OF FAME, AND PORTLAND, MAINE, NATIVE, WAS A FIRST-ROUND PICK OF THE BOSTON RED SOX IN 1974?**

A. Bob Stanley. The Steamer pitched only for the Red Sox during his thirteen-year major league career, compiling a 115–97 career record, while recording a Red Sox record of 132 saves. He is the only pitcher to register at least 100 wins and 100 saves with the Red Sox.

**Q. WHAT CHERRYFIELD RIGHT-HANDED PITCHER WAS NAMED NATIONAL LEAGUE PITCHING ROOKIE OF THE YEAR BY *THE SPORTING NEWS* IN 1958?**

A. Carlton Francis Willey. Willey pitched eight years in the major leagues for the Milwaukee Braves and New York Mets. As a rookie, he pitched in the 1958 World Series against the New York Yankees. He finished with a lifetime 38–58 record and career ERA of 3.76.

**Q. What Lawrence High School and University of Maine basketball star was a first-round draft pick of the Cleveland Rockers of the WNBA (Women's National Basketball Association) in 1998?**

A. Cindy Blodgett. Blodgett, while playing for the University of Maine Black Bears, led the nation in scoring for two consecutive seasons, averaging more than twenty-seven points per game in her sophomore and junior years.

**Q. What Newburgh native and 1995 NASCAR Winston Cup Rookie of the Year won the closest finish in NASCAR Sprint Cup series history?**

A. Ricky Craven. In 2003, Craven won the Carolina Dodge Dealers 400, beating Kurt Busch by 0.002 seconds, or mere inches. (In 2011, the record was tied at the Aaron's 499 when Jimmie Johnson beat Clint Boyer by the same margin.) Maine's Craven finished his career with two Sprint Cup wins and forty-one Top Ten Finishes. Craven is now a broadcaster with ESPN.

**Q. WHAT ST. ALBANS NATIVE BEGAN HIS MAJOR LEAGUE BASEBALL CAREER IN 1898 WITH THE BROOKLYN BRIDEGROOMS?**

A. George Henry Magoon. Magoon played for five major league teams in his five-year career as a shortstop and second baseman, finishing his career with a .239 batting average and driving in 201 runs. But the real question is, the Brooklyn Bridegrooms? Yes, the Bridegrooms. You may recognize them better by their present name—the Los Angeles Dodgers. The Bridegrooms were also known through the years as the Grooms, Superbas, Robins, and Trolley Dodgers. They became the Brooklyn Dodgers in the 1930s.

**Q. DICK MACPHERSON, FORMER HEAD COACH OF THE SYRACUSE ORANGEMEN FOOTBALL TEAM AND THE NEW ENGLAND PATRIOTS FOOTBALL TEAM, IS A NATIVE OF WHAT MAINE TOWN?**

A. Old Town.

**Q. WHAT WASHINGTON COUNTY NATIVE AND FORMER MAJOR LEAGUE BASEBALL PLAYER IS CREDITED AS THE BASEBALL SCOUT WHO SIGNED JACKIE ROBINSON?**

A. Clyde "Sukey" Sukeforth (1901–2000). Sukeforth played for the Cincinnati Reds and the Brooklyn Dodgers. He was a manager in the Dodgers farm system before his promotion to Leo Durocher's Dodgers staff in 1943, where he served as both coach and scout.

Sukeforth was the only other person in the room when Dodgers president Branch Rickey told Robinson of his plans to sign him to a contract to play in Montreal in 1946. Because Durocher was suspended at the start of the1947 season, Sukeforth actually managed Robinson's first major league game. Sukeforth turned down an offer to serve as manager for the entire year. Later, Sukeforth followed former Dodger GM

Branch Rickey to the Pittsburgh Pirates organization. There, as a coach and scout, he played a role in the Pirates' drafting of Roberto Clemente from the Dodgers' organization. He later turned down an offer to manage the Pirates. Sukeforth died in Waldoboro, in 2000.

*In 1951, when Dodgers manager Chuck Dressen needed a reliever to face the New York Giants' Bobby Thomson in the ninth inning of the decisive third game of the National League pennant playoff, Clyde Sukeforth, coaching in the Dodgers' bullpen, passed over Carl Erskine and sent in Ralph Branca, who gave up Thomson's "shot heard 'round the world."*

Q. *BANGOR DAILY NEWS* SPORTSWRITER BUD LEAVITT APPEARED IN A SERIES OF TELEVISION COMMERCIALS FOR J.J. NISSEN BREAD WITH WHAT LEGENDARY BASEBALL PLAYER?

A. The Splendid Splinter himself, Ted Williams.

Q. IN WHAT BALLPARK DOES THE DOUBLE-A PORTLAND SEA DOGS BASEBALL TEAM PLAY ITS HOME GAMES?

A. Hadlock Field.

*AYUH, THAT'S MIGHTY INTERESTING, JOHN!*

*The painting titled Game Called Because of Rain is one of Norman Rockwell's most famous works. It appeared on the cover of* The Saturday Evening Post, *published April 23, 1949. Maine's own Clyde Sukeforth is the Brooklyn player in the painting.*

**Q. SPEAKING OF THE SEA DOGS, THE TEAM IS NOW ASSOCIATED WITH THE BOSTON RED SOX ORGANIZATION. WHAT MAJOR LEAGUE TEAM WAS THE ORIGINAL PARENT OF THE SEA DOGS?**

A. Florida Marlins.

**Q. WHAT COLBY COLLEGE GRADUATE WON THIRTY-ONE GAMES FOR THE PHILADELPHIA ATHLETICS IN 1910, WHILE SETTING AN AMERICAN LEAGUE RECORD FOR MOST SHUTOUTS IN ONE SEASON?**

A. John "Jack" Coombs (1882–1957). Coombs also won three games in the 1910 World Series when Philadelphia beat the Chicago Cubs. Coombs finished his career with a 158–110 record and went on to coach the Duke University baseball team for more than twenty years. Both the Duke and Colby baseball fields are named after Coombs.

**Q. Bᴇғᴏʀᴇ ᴛʜᴇ Pᴏʀᴛʟᴀɴᴅ Sᴇᴀ Dᴏɢs, ᴡʜᴀᴛ ᴡᴀs ᴛʜᴇ ɴᴀᴍᴇ ᴏғ Mᴀɪɴᴇ's ᴘʀᴇᴠɪᴏᴜs ᴍɪɴᴏʀ ʟᴇᴀɢᴜᴇ ʙᴀsᴇʙᴀʟʟ ᴛᴇᴀᴍ?**

A. Maine Guides. The Guides were a Triple-A team that played at Old Orchard Beach and were an affiliate of the Cleveland Indians.

**Q. Bᴇғᴏʀᴇ ᴛʜᴇ Pᴏʀᴛʟᴀɴᴅ Sᴇᴀ Dᴏɢs, ᴡʜᴀᴛ ᴡᴀs ᴛʜᴇ ɴᴀᴍᴇ ᴏғ Pᴏʀᴛʟᴀɴᴅ's ᴘʀᴇᴠɪᴏᴜs ᴍɪɴᴏʀ ʟᴇᴀɢᴜᴇ ʙᴀsᴇʙᴀʟʟ ᴛᴇᴀᴍ?**

A. The Portland Pilots, in 1949.

**Q. Lᴏʙsᴛᴇʀ ғɪsʜᴇʀᴍᴀɴ Eᴅᴍᴜɴᴅ "Rɪᴘ" Bʟᴀᴄᴋ ᴏғ Bᴀɪʟᴇʏ Isʟᴀɴᴅ ᴡᴏɴ ᴛʜᴇ ʙʀᴏɴᴢᴇ ᴍᴇᴅᴀʟ ɪɴ ᴛʜᴇ 1928 Oʟʏᴍᴘɪᴄs ɪɴ Aᴍsᴛᴇʀᴅᴀᴍ ɪɴ ᴡʜᴀᴛ ᴇᴠᴇɴᴛ?**

A. The hammer throw.

**Q. Wʜᴀᴛ Lᴇᴡɪsᴛᴏɴ ɴᴀᴛɪᴠᴇ, ɴɪᴄᴋɴᴀᴍᴇᴅ "Rᴏᴜɢʜ Bɪʟʟ," ᴡᴀs ᴛʜᴇ ᴄᴀᴛᴄʜᴇʀ-ᴍᴀɴᴀɢᴇʀ ғᴏʀ ᴛʜᴇ Bᴏsᴛᴏɴ Rᴇᴅ Sᴏx, ɢᴜɪᴅɪɴɢ ᴛʜᴇ ᴛᴇᴀᴍ ᴛᴏ ᴛʜᴇ Wᴏʀʟᴅ Sᴇʀɪᴇs ᴄʜᴀᴍᴘɪᴏɴsʜɪᴘ ɪɴ ʙᴏᴛʜ 1915 ᴀɴᴅ 1916?**

A. William "Bill" Carrigan (1883–1969). Carrigan also played on the 1912 team that won the World Series and was elected to the Boston Red Sox Hall of Fame. Babe Ruth reportedly called Carrigan the best manager he ever played for.

**Q. Wʜᴀᴛ ᴛᴡᴏ-ᴛɪᴍᴇ Oʟʏᴍᴘɪᴀɴ ғʀᴏᴍ Lᴇᴡɪsᴛᴏɴ ᴡᴏɴ ᴛʜᴇ ʙʀᴏɴᴢᴇ ᴍᴇᴅᴀʟ ɪɴ ᴛʜᴇ ᴘᴇɴᴛᴀᴛʜʟᴏɴ ᴀᴛ ᴛʜᴇ 1924 Oʟʏᴍᴘɪᴄ Gᴀᴍᴇs ɪɴ Pᴀʀɪs, sᴇᴛᴛɪɴɢ ᴛʜᴇ ᴡᴏʀʟᴅ ʀᴇᴄᴏʀᴅ ғᴏʀ ᴛʜᴇ ʟᴏɴɢ ᴊᴜᴍᴘ ɪɴ ᴛʜᴇ ᴘʀᴏᴄᴇss?**

A. Robert LeGendre (1898–1931). His jump as part of the pentathlon was longer than the jump that won the gold medal in the actual long jump event.

**Q. What Portland bowler was twice world singles champion in candlepin bowling and twice named Bowler of the Year? (Hint: She was also the first woman inducted into the Maine Sports Hall of Fame.)**

A. Dot Petty.

**Q. What University of Maine baseball coach guided the Black Bears to the College World Series six times?**

A. John Winkin.

**Q. WHAT BIDDEFORD NATIVE PLAYED SHORTSTOP FOR THE 1903 RED SOX, THE RED SOX TEAM THAT WON THE FIRST EVER MAJOR LEAGUE WORLD SERIES?**

A. Freddy Parent (1875–1972). Parent played in the major leagues for eleven seasons and was mostly known for his defense, although he finished with a career batting average of .262. When he died in Sanford in 1972, he was the last surviving member of the first World Series championship team.

**Q. WHAT BREWER NATIVE WON THE SILVER MEDAL FOR SAILING IN THE 1992 OLYMPIC GAMES IN BARCELONA, SPAIN?**

A. Kevin Mahaney.

# ARTS AND LITERATURE

**Q. AUTHOR STEPHEN KING IS CLOSELY ASSOCIATED WITH THE CITY OF BANGOR, ALTHOUGH HE WAS ACTUALLY BORN IN PORTLAND. HOWEVER, HE GREW UP IN NEITHER. FROM WHAT MAINE HIGH SCHOOL DID KING GRADUATE?**

A. Lisbon Falls High School, class of 1966.

**Q. WHAT COLLEGE DID STEPHEN KING ATTEND?**

A. The University of Maine at Orono. He graduated with a BA in English, in 1970.

**Q. AT WHAT MAINE HIGH SCHOOL DID STEPHEN KING TEACH ENGLISH?**

A. Hampden Academy.

**Q. IN THE MOVIE *SHAWSHANK REDEMPTION*, BASED ON A SHORT STORY BY MAINER STEPHEN KING, TIM ROBBINS'S CHARACTER TELLS**

**MORGAN FREEMAN'S CHARACTER TO VISIT A HAYFIELD IN WHAT MAINE TOWN, TO FIND A SPECIAL PACKAGE?**

A. Buxton.

**Q. IN THE MOVIE *SHAWSHANK REDEMPTION*, WHAT WAS THE NAME OF THE CHARACTER PLAYED BY TIM ROBBINS?**

A. Andy Dufresne.

**Q. SPEAKING, AGAIN, OF STEPHEN KING: THE MOVIE *FIRESTARTER*, STARRING DREW BARRYMORE, HAD ITS WORLD PREMIERE IN WHAT MAINE CITY?**

A. Bangor.

**Q. WHICH PORTLAND NATIVE AND FAMOUS MINISTER AT CHURCHES IN HARPSWELL AND TOPSHAM WROTE SEVERAL SERIES OF POPULAR BOOKS SET IN MAINE THAT WERE AIMED AT MIDDLE SCHOOL BOYS, INCLUDING THE ELM ISLAND SERIES AND THE WHISPERING PINE SERIES?**

A. Elijah Kellogg.

**Q. WHICH PORTLAND NATIVE CREATED SUCH MAGAZINES AS *LADIES' HOME JOURNAL* AND *THE SATURDAY EVENING POST*?**

A. Cyrus Hermann Kotzschmar, founder of Curtis Publishing.

**Q. WHICH FAMOUS ARTIST SAID, "NEVER PUT MORE THAN TWO WAVES IN A PAINTING"?**

A. Winslow Homer.

**Q. WHO FOUNDED THE PORTLAND PRESS HERALD?**

A. Guy Patterson Gannett. Gannett purchased the *Portland Daily Press* and the *Portland Herald* and merged them to create the *Portland Press Herald* in 1921. In 1925, Gannett also purchased the *Evening Express and Daily Advertiser* and the *Portland Sunday Telegram*. The paper remained under family control until it was sold to The Seattle Times Company in 1998.

**Q. FOR WHOM IS ROCKLAND'S FARNSWORTH MUSEUM NAMED?**

A. William A. Farnsworth (1815–1876), a successful Rockland businessman. His daughter Lucy Farnsworth (1838–1935) directed that the bulk of the Farnsworth estate be used to establish the William A. Farnsworth Library and Art Museum as a memorial to her father. The museum officially opened in August of 1948.

### Q. WHO WAS STEPHEN EVANS MERRILL?

A. A Maine humorist best known for the 1961 recording, *Father Fell Down the Well & Other Maine Stories*. He hailed from Skowhegan and Brunswick.

### Q. SPEAKING OF MAINE HUMOR, WHO WAS HOLMAN DAY?

A. Okay, you've probably guessed he was a humorist. Very good! Born in Vassalboro in 1865, he was a poet, novelist, and filmmaker, as well as publisher and editor of the *Dexter Gazette*, and later, managing editor of the *Lewiston Evening Sun Journal*. He wrote a daily poetry column, "Up in Maine," a collection of which made up his first book. A true multimedia guy.

### Q. WHICH FORT FAIRFIELD NATIVE RECORDED THE HUGE COUNTRY HIT, "TOMBSTONE EVERY MILE," WHICH CLIMBED TO NUMBER 5 ON THE BILLBOARD CHARTS IN 1965?

A. Dick Curless (1932–1995), known as the Baron of Country Music and a pioneer of the trucking music genre. Curless recorded twenty-two songs that appeared on the Billboard Charts, including "Big Wheel Cannonball." In the late 1960s he toured with the legendary Buck Owens.

### Q. IN THE SONG, "TOMBSTONE EVERY MILE," CURLESS SAYS IF YOU'RE HAULIN' GOODS, YOU'D RATHER BE ANYWHERE ELSE BUT WHERE?

A. The Hainesville Woods.

**Q. STAYING ON TOPIC, CAN YOU RECITE THE REFRAIN FROM THAT FAMOUS SONG?**

A.      *It's a stretch of road up north in Maine*
        *That's never, ever, ever seen a smile*
        *If they buried all the truckers lost in them woods*
        *There'd be a tombstone every mile*
        *Count 'em off, there'd be a tombstone every mile.*

**Q. WHICH TWO FICTIONAL MAINE FISHERMEN POPULARIZED THE SAYING, "YOU CAN'T GET THERE FROM HERE"?**

A. Bert and I.

**Q. WHICH TWO YALE STUDENTS CREATED THE FICTIONAL COMEDY DUO BERT AND I?**

A. Marshall Dodge and Robert Bryan.

*AYUH, THAT'S MIGHTY INTERESTING, JOHN!*

*R*eginald Holmes of Jay was a poet who wrote more than 300 verses for greeting cards. If alive, I'm sure he'd be "thinking of you today."

**Q. IN THE ORIGINAL BERT AND I STORY, WHAT WAS THE NAME OF THE BOAT?**

A. The *Bluebird.*

**Q. IN THE 1970S, MARSHALL DODGE STARRED IN A TELEVISION SHOW THAT AIRED ON MAINE PUBLIC BROADCASTING. CAN YOU NAME THE SHOW?**

A. *A Downeast Smile-In.*

**Q. WHICH MAINE HUMORIST AND SINGER STARRED IN THE MAINE PUBLIC BROADCASTING SHOW CALLED *IN THE KITCHEN*?**

A. Kendall Morse.

**Q. WHO WROTE THE NOW-CLASSIC BOOK OF MAINE HUMOR, *A MOOSE AND A LOBSTER WALK INTO A BAR . . .***

A. John McDonald. Hey! I know, shameless!

**Q. IN WHAT FICTIONAL MAINE TOWN WAS THE POPULAR TELEVISION SHOW, *MURDER, SHE WROTE*, SET?**

A. Cabot Cove, a supposedly quiet New England town that actually had the highest murder rate in the country.

**Q. FROM WHAT FICTIONAL TOWN DID THE CHARACTER HAWKEYE PIERCE FROM THE BOOK, MOVIE AND TELEVISION SHOW, *M\*A\*S\*H*, HAIL?**

A. Crabapple Cove.

**Q. WHICH FAMOUS POET, RAISED IN GARDINER, USED THAT TOWN AS A MODEL FOR HIS "TILLBURY TOWN" POEMS?**

A. Edwin Arlington Robinson, born in Alna in 1869.

**Q. WHICH FAMOUS MAINE HUMORIST WROTE A WEEKLY COLUMN FOR *THE CHRISTIAN SCIENCE MONITOR* FOR MORE THAN SIXTY YEARS?**

A. John Gould. Gould wrote from a farm in Lisbon Falls, and later from Friendship. He also wrote thirty humorous books about Maine, including *Farmer Takes a Wife* and *The Fastest Hound Dog in the State of Maine.*

**Q. WHICH WRITER SAID HE FOUND MAINE'S WOODS, "MOOSEY AND MOSSY"?**

A. Henry David Thoreau. We assume Maine woodsmen who met Thoreau had a few clever words to say about him, but those quotes have not survived.

**Q. CAPE ELIZABETH NATIVE SEAN ALOYSIUS O'FEARNA IS BETTER KNOWN BY WHAT NAME?**

A. John Ford (1894–1973). The legendary filmmaker graduated from Portland High School and soon headed west to make movies. He directed more than eighty films and won four Academy Awards for Best Director. He was perhaps best known for his westerns, which included *Stagecoach* and *The Searchers*, both starring John Wayne. He won an Academy Award for directing John Steinbeck's *The Grapes of Wrath*.

**Q. WHO WAS SAMUEL LONGFELLOW?**

A. Younger brother of Henry Wadsworth Longfellow. Henry was a Unitarian minister and composer of many hymns. He also wrote a biography of his famous brother.

**Q. WHICH WELL-KNOWN NINETEENTH-CENTURY AMERICAN AUTHOR SPENT HIS TEENAGE YEARS LIVING IN RAYMOND AND LATER ATTENDED BOWDOIN COLLEGE, WHERE HE WAS A CLASSMATE OF FUTURE PRESIDENT FRANKLIN PIERCE AND POET HENRY WADSWORTH LONGFELLOW?**

A. Nathaniel Hawthorne (1804–1864), author of *The Scarlet Letter*.

**Q. WHICH FORMER CONTRIBUTOR TO *THE NEW YORKER* MOVED TO NORTH BROOKLIN, MAINE, WHERE HE WROTE CLASSIC CHILDREN'S BOOKS?**

A. Elwyn Brooks (E. B.) White, whose books included *Charlotte's Web*, *Stuart Little*, and *The Trumpet of the Swan*.

**Q. WHAT PLAY, SET IN VEAZIE, AND WRITTEN BY MAINE NATIVE OWEN DAVIS, WON THE 1923 PULITZER PRIZE FOR DRAMA?**

A. *Snowbound*.

**Q. WHICH ARTIST, NOTED FOR HIS LARGE-SCALE PAINTINGS INSPIRED BY THE DEEP WOODS OF MAINE, LIVED IN LINCOLNVILLE?**

A. Neil Welliver (1929–2005).

**Q. WHO PAINTED *CHRISTINA'S WORLD*, ONE OF THE BEST-KNOWN PAINTINGS IN AMERICAN HISTORY?**

A. Andrew Wyeth.

**Q. WHERE IS THE HOUSE DEPICTED IN *CHRISTINA'S WORLD* LOCATED?**

A. Known as the Olson House, it's located in Cushing.

*The woman featured in Wyeth's famous painting is Christina Olson, who was stricken with polio, a disease that paralyzed her lower body. Wyeth was inspired to create the painting when through a window from within the house he saw her crawling across a field.*

**Q. WHICH BRUNSWICK NATIVE AND RHODES SCHOLAR WROTE *STRANGE HOLINESS*, WHICH WON THE PULITZER PRIZE FOR POETRY IN 1936?**

A. Robert P. Tristram Coffin (1892–1955), a Bowdoin College professor with degrees from Bowdoin, Princeton, and Oxford, who wrote more than three dozen books of literature, poetry, and history.

**Q. Which Rockland native won the Pulitzer Prize for Poetry in 1923 for "The Ballad of the Harp-Weaver"?**

A. Edna St. Vincent Millay (1892–1950).

**Q. Which former Colby College professor and current Camden resident received the 2002 Pulitzer Prize for Fiction for his Maine-based novel, *Empire Falls*?**

A. Richard Russo.

**Q. Which Alna native, raised in Gardiner, won the Pulitzer Prize for Poetry three times: in 1922 for his first *Collected Poems*; in 1925 for *The Man Who Died Twice*; and in 1928, for *Tristram*?**

A. Edwin Arlington Robinson.

**Q. Which Kennebunk native and former *Saturday Evening Post* writer won a Pulitzer Prize Special Citation, "for his historical novels which have long contributed to the creation of greater interest in our early American history."**

A. Kenneth Roberts (1885–1957), whose works included *Arundel, Rabble in Arms,* and *Northwest Passage.*

**Q. Which Portland-born nineteenth-century poet was considered the most influential poet of his day, writing such classics as "Evangeline," "The Courtship of Miles Standish," and "Paul Revere's Ride"?**

A. Henry Wadsworth Longfellow (1807–1882).

*AYUH, THAT'S MIGHTY INTERESTING, JOHN!*

*Waterford native Charles Farrar Browne (1834–1867) was President Abraham Lincoln's favorite humorist. Browne adopted the pen name Artemus Ward, and achieved great popularity in America and England. In fact, before unveiling "The Emancipation Proclamation" to his cabinet, Lincoln read them Ward's "High-Handed Outrage at Utiky," which is said to have outraged some of the humorless members of his Cabinet. Ward also inspired Mark Twain. He died of tuberculosis while on a tour of England in 1867. He was only thirty-three.*

**Q. WHAT POPULAR MAINE PERFORMER IS PERHAPS BETTER KNOWN AS IDA LECLAIR, THE LEAD CHARACTER FROM HER PLAY, *IDA: WOMAN WHO RUNS WITH THE MOOSE*?**

A. Susan Poulin.

**Q. WHAT SON OF WESTBROOK STARRED IN THE ORIGINAL BROADWAY PRODUCTION OF *HOW TO SUCCEED IN BUSINESS WITHOUT REALLY TRYING*?**

A. Rudy Vallee, who was offered the part of J. B. Biggley after British actor Terry Thomas turned it down.

**Q. ACCORDING TO LEGEND, PRESIDENT ABRAHAM LINCOLN REPORT-EDLY SAID THIS UPON MEETING WHICH MAINE AUTHOR: "SO YOU ARE**

THE LITTLE WOMAN WHO WROTE THE BOOK THAT STARTED THIS GREAT WAR"?

A. Harriet Beecher Stowe, who wrote *Uncle Tom's Cabin*.

Q. HARRIET BEECHER STOWE WROTE *UNCLE TOM'S CABIN* WHILE LIVING IN WHAT MAINE TOWN?

A. Brunswick.

Q. WHAT MEMBER OF THE 1960S TRIO, PETER, PAUL AND MARY, NOW LIVES IN THE HANCOCK COUNTY TOWN OF BLUE HILL?

A. Noel Paul Stookey.

Q. WHAT FAMOUS ROCK STAR DIED JUST DAYS BEFORE HE WAS SCHEDULED TO PERFORM AT THE CUMBERLAND COUNTY CIVIC CENTER?

A. Elvis Presley. The King was scheduled to perform on August 18, 1977, but died on August 16.

Q. WHAT BUCKFIELD NATIVE AND BOWDOIN COLLEGE GRADUATE CREATED THE CHARACTER MAJOR JACK DOWNING, AND IS CREDITED WITH BEING ONE OF THE FIRST HUMORISTS TO USE AMERICAN VERNACULAR IN HUMOR?

A. Seba Smith (1792–1868), a newspaper editor and humorist who some consider the father of Down East humor, because of his dry, satirical style. He influenced later humorists, including Artemus Ward.

Q. THIS BLUE HILL NATIVE WROTE THE NOVEL *SILAS CROCKETT*, CONSIDERED ONE OF THE MOST IMPORTANT BOOKS IN MAINE HISTORY.

A. Mary Ellen Chase. Her other novels of the Maine coast include *Mary Peters* and *Windswept*.

**Q. Which famous Georgetown island artist is also an accomplished children's book author and illustrator whose books include *The Cat at Night* and *My Wonderful Christmas Tree*?**

A. Dahlov Ipcar.

**Q. The 1948 film, *Deep Waters*, was filmed on location in Vinalhaven and nominated for an Academy Award. It was based on what New York Times–bestselling book, by what Maine author?**

A. *Spoonhandle* by Ruth Moore. Moore, born on Gotts Island, also wrote *The Weir, Candlemas Bay*, and other novels set on the Maine coast.

**Q. Which Maine author's most popular novels were set on fictional Bennett's Island?**

A. Elisabeth Ogilvie. She wrote more than forty novels, including the Tide Trilogy: *High Tide at Noon, Storm Tide*, and *The Ebbing Tide*, all set on Bennett's Island (inspired by the real-life island of Criehaven).

**Q. What actor, born in Lewiston and raised in Buckfield, starred as neurosurgeon Dr. Derek Shepherd on the television show, *Grey's Anatomy*?**

A. Patrick Dempsey.

**Q. WHAT MAINE NATIVE IS MARRIED TO ACTRESS MICHELLE PFEIFFER, AND WHOSE FIRST FILM SCRIPT WAS *FROM THE HIP*?**

A. David E. Kelley.

**Q. WHAT PORTLAND NATIVE STARRED IN THE 1980S MOVIES *ST. ELMO'S FIRE* AND *THE BREAKFAST CLUB*?**

A. Judd Nelson.

**Q. WHAT PORTLAND NATIVE APPEARED IN THE TV SHOW *BARNEY MILLER*, AND STARRED AS ALICE HYATT ON THE TV SITCOM, *ALICE*. (HINT: SHE ALSO WON A TONY FOR HER PERFORMANCE IN NEIL SIMON'S *BROADWAY BOUND*.)**

A. Linda Lavin.

**Q. WHAT LEWISTON ARTIST IS CONSIDERED ONE OF AMERICA'S BEST MODERNIST PAINTERS, WHO PAINTED SOME OF HIS MOST FAMOUS WORKS—INCLUDING *EVENING STORM* AND *LOBSTER FISHERMAN*—WHILE LIVING IN MAINE? HE DIED IN ELLSWORTH IN 1943, AT THE AGE OF SIXTY-SIX.**

A. Marsden Hartley (1877–1943).

# PLACES

**Q. WHAT MAINE CITY IS KNOWN AS THE CITY OF SHIPS?**

A. Bath.

**Q. HOW DO MANY RESIDENTS OF PORTLAND REFER TO THE CITY'S TWO MAIN SECTIONS?**

A. "Place with many coffee shops" and "place with fewer coffee shops." No, seriously, Portland's two distinct areas are "on-peninsula" and "off-peninsula."

**Q. WHERE IS THE SARAH MILDRED LONG BRIDGE, AND HOW DID IT GET ITS NAME?**

A. The Sarah M. Long Bridge is a lift bridge that carries Route 1 traffic across the Piscataquis River, which serves as the border between New Hampshire and Maine. The bridge was named in honor of Sarah Mildred Long, who was an employee of the

113

Maine–New Hampshire Bridge Authority for more than fifty years.

### Q. HOW DID PORTLAND'S MILLION DOLLAR BRIDGE GET ITS NAME?

A. The story goes that when they started building the bridge across the Fore River, between Portland and South Portland, back in 1915, the cost of the bridge kept climbing and climbing until people started saying, "We've got ourselves a million-dollar bridge right there, whether we wanted one or not." That's the story we came up with after "researching" the question. If you've got a better story we'd love to hear it. The bridge was demolished in 1997–1998.

### Q. WHERE IS MAINE'S MOST FAMOUS CRIBSTONE BRIDGE?

A. The last time anyone checked, it was stretched between Bailey and Orr's islands.

### Q. WHERE IS NORTH AMERICA'S ONLY FJORD?

A. We realize that this answer won't determine the rise and fall of nations, but there seems to be some question about Mount Desert Island's claim that they have North America's only fjord, in Somes Sound. Some fjord fans disagree. What's the truth? We're sticking behind MDI's assertion. And, before we go further—please, we've heard all the jokes: Mount Desert Island has plenty of fjords, as well as Chevys and Caddies.

### Q. HOW DID CHRISTMAS COVE GET ITS NAME?

A. Explorer John Smith anchored in the cove on Christmas Day in 1604, and decided to call the quaint cove after the day. Granted, if named today, it would probably be called Happy Holiday Cove.

**Q. What and where is the Wedding Cake House?**

A. The Wedding Cake House is located at 104 Summer Street in Kennebunk. Shipbuilder George W. Bourne built the house in 1825, and it's now called "the most photographed house in Maine." No, I've never photographed it, and don't know anyone who has, but apparently a lot of people have. Feel free to snap a few pictures yourself, if you like.

**Q. What is the proper way to pronounce the name of this Maine coastal town: Calais?**

A. Calais is pronounced KAL-iss, never, ever Cal-LAY.

*That reminds me of a Maine mixed-marriage couple—he was native, she was from away—who were driving to Calais to visit his relatives. He told his wife not to call the town Cal-LAY while they were there; she'd only make a fool of herself.*

*Well, they argued on and off all the way down the coast. (In Maine, when going from Portland to Calais, you're going down the coast. Going from Calais to Portland, it's up the coast. Don't argue. That's just the way it is.)*

*Anyway, as soon as they went over the town line the husband swerved into the parking lot of the first business they came to. He told his wife to come with him into the business and they'd straighten this thing out once and for all.*

*They walked up to the counter and the husband said to the clerk: "Will you please tell my wife where we are?"*

*The clerk said: "Dunkin' Donuts."*

**Q. WHAT TOWN IN MAINE WAS ONCE CONSIDERED "THE SARDINE CAPITAL OF THE WORLD"?**

A. Eastport. In the late nineteenth century, Eastport boasted thirteen large sardine-canning factories operating twenty-four hours a day, seven days a week, during the season. Today, there are no canning operations in Eastport.

AYUH, THAT'S MIGHTY INTERESTING, JOHN!

*They say you can't pick your relatives, or the founder of your town. Carmel, a Penobscot County town—named for the biblical Mount Carmel—was founded by Reverend George Higgins, a renegade Methodist minister and founder of a faith-healing sect known for bizarre ceremonies, including anti-satanic child-flogging. Carmelites finally had enough, dragged him from his home, tarred and feathered him, and drove him out of town. But they liked the name he gave their town, so they kept it. Reverend Higgins got the hint from the tarring and feathering, and never returned to Carmel.*

**Q. WHEN ARE THE EARLIEST AND LATEST "ICE-OUT" DATES—THE DATES THAT ICE WAS DECLARED OUT OF MOOSEHEAD LAKE?**

A. The term "ice-out" doesn't mean that all the ice in the lake has melted; it just means that a boat can travel from one end of the lake to the other without being blocked by ice. Since they started keeping track, the earliest was April 14, in 1945. The latest date was May 29, in 1878.

**Q. WHAT U.S. ROAD, LAID OUT IN THE 1920S, STRETCHES FROM FORT KENT AT THE NORTHERN TIP OF MAINE ALL THE WAY TO KEY WEST, FLORIDA?**

A. U.S. Route 1. The border town of Fort Kent is named for the fort built there on the Maine-Canadian border. The fort and the town are named for Edward Kent, a Maine governor. You'll have to ask someone in Florida how Key West got its name.

**Q. WHAT MAINE VILLAGE IS CONSIDERED THE HIGHEST IN THE STATE?**

A. Paris Hill, which is 831 feet above sea level—as high as any Maine town ought to be. The historic village was Oxford County's first shire town, and the birthplace of Hannibal Hamlin, Abraham Lincoln's first vice president. The Hamlin Memorial Library and Museum is housed in what was the Oxford County jail.

**Q. EDEN WAS THE ORIGINAL NAME OF WHAT MAINE TOWN?**

A. Bar Harbor.

**Q. WHAT WAS THE ORIGINAL NAME OF ACADIA NATIONAL PARK?**

A. Lafayette National Park.

**Q. THE FILM, *THE MAN WITHOUT A FACE*, WAS FILMED IN WHAT MIDCOAST TOWN?**

A. Camden was the primary location for the film, starring and directed by Mel Gibson. The story was based on Isabelle Holland's 1972 novel of the same name. The movie was released in 1993.

**Q. WHERE IN MAINE DID THE FIRST TRANSATLANTIC BALLOON FLIGHT BEGIN?**

A. Presque Isle. Double Eagle II, piloted by Ben Abruzzo, Maxie Anderson, and Larry Newman, became the first balloon to cross the Atlantic Ocean in 1978, when it landed in Miserey, near Paris, after a flight of 137 hours and 6 minutes.

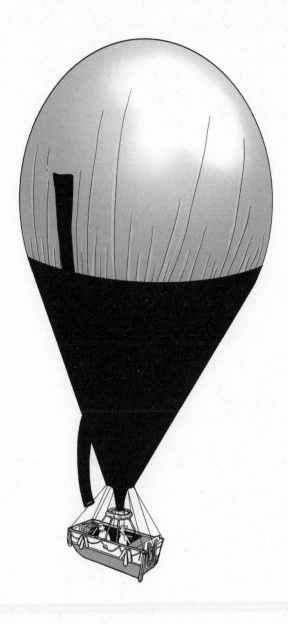

### Q. WHAT MAINE CITY HAS THE MOST COLLEGES OR UNIVERSITIES?

A. Bangor boasts six: Beal College, Bangor Theological Seminary, Eastern Maine Community College, Husson University, and New England School of Communications. Portland and Lewiston are tied for second, with five each.

### Q. FOR WHAT SPECIFIC PURPOSE WAS FORT KNOX BUILT?

A. Even as late as 1844, it was felt that a fort was needed on the Penobscot River to protect the Penobscot River Valley from a British naval attack. The fort was made from granite cut from nearby Mount Waldo.

### Q. WHY ARE THE INITIALS TO PORTLAND'S INTERNATIONAL JETPORT "PWM"?

A. Because its original name was Portland-Westbrook Municipal.

> *The Portland Jetport, of course, is not the only airstrip in Maine. I once heard that back during World War II, the government built an emergency landing strip Down East for B-17s and other big bombers that needed an emergency landing field after flying across the North Atlantic.*
>
> *After the war, the town's selectmen decided to make a commercial airfield out of the strip, because they were told that a town would never get anywhere in the modern world unless it had an airport. All tourists want the option of flying to a destination, they were told. So, the town manager sent out requests for proposals to all the big airlines—Delta, TWA, American—but not a single one responded.*
>
> *About six months later the selectmen received a reply from a little-known airline called Old Buzzard, whose motto was: "Nothing scares us."*

*The terse reply made it clear that the company was anxious to become part of the Greater Cherryfield experience. Having no other takers, the town fathers let them open a ticket window and begin regular service to various towns in and out of Maine.*

*The most immediate effect of the new service was a drop in betting on the trotters at the Cherryfield Fair that summer. Instead of betting $10 or $20 at the track, people were going to the Old Buzzard ticket window and saying: "I'd like to take a chance on Flight 24 to Presque Isle." Them airline tickets were a bit more expensive, but the game was a lot more sporting.*

**Q. L.L. BEAN IN FREEPORT WAS FOUNDED IN FREEPORT IN 1912, AND HAS BECOME SYNONYMOUS WITH MAINE. WHAT ORIGINAL PRODUCT IS CREDITED WITH BUILDING THE BEAN EMPIRE?**

A. The Maine Hunting Shoe, better known simply as the Bean Boot.

**Q WHAT DO THE INITIALS "L.L." IN L.L. BEAN STAND FOR?**

A. Leon Leonwood.

**Q. TRUE OR FALSE: THE MAIN DOORS OF THE L.L. BEAN FLAGSHIP STORE IN FREEPORT DO NOT HAVE ANY LOCKS.**

A. True.

**Q. IN THE MOVIE *THE PREACHER'S WIFE*, STARRING WHITNEY HOUSTON AND DENZEL WASHINGTON, WHERE IN MAINE WAS THE ICE-SKATING SCENE FILMED?**

A. On the frozen duck pond in Portland's Deering Oaks Park.

**Q. WHERE IS THE LAST ACTIVE SHAKER COMMUNITY IN THE UNITED STATES?**

A. Sabbathday Lake, in New Gloucester, Maine.

**Q. WHERE DID THE GRANITE COME FROM TO BUILD THE MONUMENT TO GENERAL ULYSSES S. GRANT ON RIVERSIDE DRIVE IN NEW YORK CITY?**

A. North Jay (the same town where my wife and I once bought a beautiful Duchess Atlantic woodstove).

**Q. SPEAKING OF BEAUTIFUL GRANITE, WHERE DID THE GRANITE FOR THE TOWERS AND APPROACHES OF NEW YORK'S TRIBOROUGH BRIDGE COME FROM?**

A. Vinalhaven Island.

**Q. WHILE WE'RE ON THE SUBJECT, HOW MANY GRANITE QUARRIES WERE BEING WORKED IN MAINE AT THE END OF THE NINETEENTH CENTURY?**

A. More than 100.

**Q. WHERE DOES THE APPALACHIAN TRAIL CROSS INTO MAINE?**

A. In the Mahoosuc Mountains, northwest of Bethel, near where Route 26 crosses into New Hampshire.

**Q. WHAT HISTORIC PREP SCHOOL IS LOCATED IN THE WESTERN TOWN OF BETHEL?**

A. Gould Academy.

**Q. WHAT SKI RESORT DID LES OTTEN PURCHASE IN THE MID-1980S AND BUILD INTO ONE OF NEW ENGLAND'S MOST SUCCESSFUL SKI DESTINATIONS?**

A. Sunday River.

**Q. WHAT LAKE (MAINE'S FOURTH LARGEST) WAS CREATED, AND WHAT TOWN OF THE SAME NAME WAS FLOODED AND DESTROYED IN 1949, WHEN CENTRAL MAINE POWER COMPANY DAMMED THE DEAD RIVER?**

A. Flagstaff Lake.

**Q. WHERE MIGHT ONE GO IN YARMOUTH IF ONE GOT LOST?**

A. DeLorme, a world-renowned map company that has been telling people where to go (in a nice way) for more than thirty years. I'm sure some frustrated motorists are happy to have better maps than to have to rely on locals for directions.

> My old friend Tewkey Merrill was sitting on his front porch reading the newspaper one day when a car came tearing around the corner by his house and stopped. A man jumps from the car, runs up onto the porch, and frantically asks Tewkey for directions to Bangor.
> Realizing the fella is in a hurry, Tewkey tries his best to move him right along.
> "You want to take this road out of town about five miles and you're gonna come to a fork in the road . . ."
> "Does it make any difference which way I go at the fork?" the stranger asks, thinking he'll speed things up.
> "Not to me, it don't," Tewkey says, honestly.
> The stranger decides to just stand there and listen.
> "You take a left at that fork, and after you go another two miles you'll see a big, red barn. No, come to think of it, it's a green barn . . . Two miles after that left at the fork in the road, you'll see a big, green barn."
> Tewkey paused again to think, while the stranger tapped his foot, waiting.
> "Now that I've colored the barn green I realize it's not on the left side but on the right side," says Tewkey. "So, remember—two

miles after the left at the fork in the road on your right-hand side, you're going see a big, green . . ."

Another long pause, more thinking. The stranger is fit to be tied.

"For the last eight years that barn's been nothing but trouble," Tewkey finally said. "Eight years ago the fella who owns that barn decided to paint it even though it didn't need painting. In the middle of the job he gets a call from his daughter in Canton, Ohio, who just had her first baby. Well, he and Mother pack up and fly

to Canton to see their new grandchild. They stay out there for months, visiting. By the time they got back he couldn't remember whether his barn was red and he'd been painting it green, or she was green and he'd been painting it red. What's worse, he couldn't find any of the paint.

"His neighbor, Frank Farron, said, 'Just wait till one side starts peeling. Whatever side peels first is probably the side you painted first, so just paint that side the other color.'

126

*"Fella agreed that was the answer. Trouble is, till he finishes painting his barn I can't remember—when giving directions—whether his barn is the red barn on the left heading north or she's the green barn on the right heading south.*

*"But I know for sure that two miles after the left at the fork in the road, on either your left-or right-hand side, I guarantee you're going to see a big red or green barn," Tewkey said, all emphatic.*

*"Then what do I do?" the stranger asked.*

*"Nothin'," said Tewkey. "You see it and just go sailing by."*

**Q. DELORME IS HOME TO THE LARGEST OF THESE IN THE WORLD. WHAT IS IT?**

A. A globe, named Eartha.

**Q. THE MAINE MARITIME MUSEUM IS BUILT ON THE SITE OF WHAT FAMOUS KENNEBEC RIVER SHIPYARD?**

A. Percy & Small, which built the largest wooden ship ever built in the United States—the 450-foot, six-masted *Wyoming*.

**Q. HOW DID THE *WYOMING* GET ITS NAME?**

A. One of the owners was Bryant Butler Brooks, who was governor of *Wyoming* at the time.

The *Wyoming* was built in 1909 at the staggering cost of $175,000. The ship was 450 feet from jib boom to spanker boom tip. It still has the distinction of being the largest wooden sailing vessel ever built. The *Wyoming* was equipped with a state-of-the-art Maine-built Hyde windlass to haul it, a massive anchor, and a donkey steam engine to haul and lower its sails.

The donkey engine allowed the *Wyoming* to be sailed with a smaller crew of only eleven hands.

Because it was so long and made of wood, the *Wyoming* tended to flex in heavy seas. The flexing caused the long planks to twist and buckle, which allowed seawater to pour into the hold—something all sailors know is never good. Her crew had to use pumps to keep its hold as free of water as possible.

In March of 1924, the *Wyoming* foundered in heavy seas and sank with the loss of all hands.

*W*. S. Wells & Sons in Wilton, Maine, is the only cannery in the world to pack dandelion greens. Under the brand name "Belle of Maine," it is also the only cannery in the U.S. to pack fiddlehead greens and beet greens.

### Q. FOR WHOM IS BATH'S CARLTON BRIDGE NAMED?

A. Frank W. Carlton, a state senator from Woolwich, who in 1925 introduced legislation to fund the bridge. How badly did the people in the Bath area want to replace the ferry with a modern bridge? Well, the vote on the referendum question to issue the state bonds to pay for the span was 2,800 "yes" votes to 103 "no" votes. Although named for Senator Carlton, the original idea for the bridge came from Luther Maddocks of Boothbay Harbor.

**Q. What do the letters "B" and "M" stand for in B&M Baked Beans?**

A. Burnham & Morrill. The company started in Portland, Maine, in 1867.

# FINAL ROUND: BONUS QUESTIONS

### Q. WHY IS MAINE LOCATED "DOWN EAST?"

A. Buckle up, this is going to take some 'splaining. Even now in the twenty-first century there's a lot that's still murky about the ubiquitous word, or words, "Downeast" or "Down East" as some would have it. We still can't agree on whether it's a single word or a two-word phrase. And that's just the beginning of the problem.

A question you often get from summer complaints is: "How come they call a place that looks like it's 'up north' 'Down East'?" It's a good question, and I'm sure there are all kinds of clever, sarcastic answers we could come up with here, but for the time being we'll try and avoid the temptation. To get the actual answer you have to go back to the nineteenth century when most everything in and out of Maine arrived and departed on sailing vessels.

To sailors heading out of Boston the easiest trip you could take was a sail down to Maine, since the prevailing winds along the New England coast were most-often from the southwest to the northeast. If you were on a schooner sailing from Boston to Maine you could expect a pleasant down-wind sail to the northeast. To continue this, you could say that the least popular voyage for nineteenth century sailors was an up-wind sail from Down East to Boston.

When a sailor in Boston was asked where they were off to he might say he was heading to Maine. But rather than drag the whole thing out and say I'm taking a down-wind sail to the Northeast, he would simply say I'm heading Down East.

Even when I was a kid back in the Sixties my grandfather would insist that if you were going to a ball game at Fenway Park you were going "up" to Boston and when the game was over you'd leave Boston and come back "down" to Maine.

So, it all goes back to the days when schooners ruled the waves in these parts and many of the phrases of sailors became the phrases of Maine—and yes I do know all the implications of that statement.

**Q. WHERE DOES DOWN EAST BEGIN?**

A. Trick question. No one really knows.

Sailors in the old days considered it to be any destination from Maine to the Maritime Provinces of Canada. I once asked a new arrival to Portland if they'd ever been Down East and he matter-of-factly stated: "I've been to Freeport." Now, most everyone would admit that Freeport has more claim to the designation Down East than Fryberg but just barely.

Most people in Portland and further south agree that you're not really Down East until you get up to about Bath, the ship-building town on the Kennebec. In Bath you might be told that you have to go beyond Thomaston to Rockland if you want to get the feel for Down East.

In Rockland they're likely to laugh right in your face and then tell you to keep on truckin' because you won't even get a good whiff of Down East until you get to the former broiler capital of the world—Belfast.

By now you should begin to catch on so you won't even stop in Belfast you'll just keep going. In Searsport you might stop and someone there will tell you that you're getting closer, but

that you'll have to get east of fashionable Ellsworth before you're in the vicinity of Down East.

This will go on and on until you finally find yourself in the visitor parking lot at West Quoddy Head Light, the eastern most point of land in the United States. Then you'll scratch your head and wonder—as many have wondered before you—why is the easternmost point of land Down East called WEST Quoddy Head?

**Q. IN WHAT MONTH WAS THE "TRADITIONAL" TOWN MEETING HELD?**

A. March.

If the traditional New England town meeting didn't exist we here in Maine would have to invent it just to add a tad of excitement to our lives at this thrill-challenged time of year. They say when our colonial ancestors first started experiment-ing with the town meeting concept they tried scheduling their meetings in other months, but after a long period of trial and error New England towns finally settled on March because, as they rightly observed, March is unquestionably the most use-less stretch of days ever to occur on a calendar made by humans.

Think about it. What else is there for decent hardworking citi-zens in Maine to do in the dreary month of March but sit around a heat-challenged town hall for three or four hours and argue with neighbors about the condition of the town's roads and how much should be spent to make them passable? Even those rare towns among us that are inhabited only by enlight-ened citizens and therefore usually have no known problems can easily conjure up one or two in March, when the rotten weather has a way of making even the most ideal situations worse than what they really are.

Those who are into conspiracies—and who isn't these days— like to think that town meetings were set in March by ruthless town road commissioners. They argue that no one in their right mind would vote against a road budget, however bloated, after riding over a few miles of the town's disintegrating roads. The ride to town meeting in March is argument to spend whatever it'll take to get the roads back in shape.

It's also said that anyone in Maine still in their right mind makes plans to be enjoying the sunny climes of our country's southern regions about the time March arrives in Maine. So just who's voting at these town meetings, anyway?

Some of Maine's trendy towns—with no respect for stodgy New England tradition—have abandoned March meetings altogether and now have their town meetings in unsuitable months like July, or worse yet, August. But, in March, we're much less likely to be busy with pesky out-of-state visitors and more likely to attend. Also, you can't work in the woods in March because of mud season, and for the same reason you couldn't do much plowing or planting in your fields, either. What better time to get together and get all the town's unpleasant business out of the way before the nice weather arrives?

Back home when I was a kid the town manager who planned our March meetings was Amos Mathews. At selectmen's meetings when asked a question like: "How many people work for the town these days, Amos?" He would scratch his head and say something like: "I'd say hardly any of them." Amos also had a framed needlepoint hanging on the wall behind his desk. It read: "So little time; so little to do. He was a true town employee.

I heard recently that Amos finally retired and they're planning to name the town hall's new wing after him. Selectmen have hired a new town manager from away named Fred Clark, who says he plans to tear up the pea patch there in town and finally get some things done.

I just hope he doesn't reschedule March meeting. The town needs all the excitement it can get at this time of year.

**Q. SHOULD YOU PAY THE ASKING PRICE MAKING A PURCHASE AT A YARD SALE IN MAINE?**

A. Heavens, No!

In late spring, Yard Sale season begins with sale items blooming like dandelions on lawns across Maine.

As this robust state industry awakens to another exciting season of wild, sometimes raucous, completely unregulated and untaxed retail activity—a Libertarian's dream—I thought it would be a good idea to review some of its unique customs, just so you won't be embarrassed by committing a yard sale faux pas. Note that I said "customs." There are no rules for yard sales—that would smack of regulation—but you should know that in yard sale society, "customs" are to be strictly observed.

As you begin your first yard sale tour of the season there are some things you should keep in mind. First, whenever possible, you should always make your yard sale experience part of a tour. A visit to several sales gives you more variety—and variety is the spice of life. Oh, that reminds me of something else: Never buy spices at a yard sale. I can't remember exactly why you shouldn't, but, as I recall it, there are good reasons.

According to custom, yard sales are made up of items that come very close to being thrown on the town dump or transferred to one of our many modern transfer stations. That's because before any yard sale a family will go through the stacks of stuff they want to get rid of and make two piles, one for the dump, another item for the yard sale. Often, it's a close call. Comments such as, "Oh, throw it on the yard sale pile for now; we can always take it to the dump later," are common during yard sale preparation. The point is, most of the stuff in the average yard sale is pretty close to being worthless. So, anything a family can get from a yard sale is considered "found money."

Another thing to know about yard sales is that when the signs say 8 a.m. to 4 p.m. you shouldn't come pounding on the door at quarter to six in the morning. Early birds are assumed to be dealers and they're difficult enough to deal with at any hour of the day but most difficult before 6 a.m.

Almost as bad are members of the eBay crowd, who like to scour a yard sale or two before breakfast and post a few dozen items online before lunch. Then, while you're slaving away in your yard, the eBayers are sitting with their laptops in the wireless coffee shop down the street keeping track of the bidding on their precious items.

But back to yard sales and the people who visit them.

When you see a worthless item priced at $10 sitting before you on a lawn, you should never just whip out a ten and hand it to the yard sale host and move on. In yard sale circles it is considered a violation of yard sale etiquette to pay the asking price for any item, without first giving your host an opportunity to hone his or her haggling skills.

And one more thing. Although yard sales are serious business here in Maine you should try and have fun at the sales you visit, and please don't text me bragging about how much you made selling your yard sale finds on eBay.

# ACKNOWLEDGMENTS

There have been many, many wonderful books written about the great state of Maine in general and even more dealing with specific aspects of Maine history. And in 2012, there are also many wonderful websites that also offer great information. My editors and I used many of these sources to research this book.

The books we reviewed included: *Maine; a Bicentenial History* by Charles E. Clark; *Maine Almanac* by Jim Brunelle; *Maine; a literary chronicle* by W. Storrs Lee; *Maine Trivia* by John N. Cole; *Enjoying Maine* by Bill Caldwell; *Rivers of Fortune* by Bill Caldwell; *Maine My First Pocket Guide* by Carole Marsh; *Yankee Talk* by Robert Hendrickson; *It Happened in Maine* by Gail Underwood Parker; *The Maine Reader: The Down East Experience from 1614 to the Present*, edited by Charles and Samuella Shain; *A Distant War Comes Home: Maine in the Civil War Era*, edited by Donald W. Beattie, Rodney M. Cole, and Charles G. Waugh; *Maine: A Narrative History* by Neil Rolde; *The Story of Bangor: A*

*Brief History of Maine's Queen City*, published by BookMarc's Publishing; *Maine: The Pine Tree State from Prehistory to the Present*, edited by Richard W. Judd, Edwin A. Churchill, and Joel W. Eastman; *Maine: Downeast and Different* by Neil Rolde.

In addition, we visited various websites including the websites developed by the state of Maine (www.maine.gov) and many Maine towns, such as lubec.mainememory.net. We also used entries that appear as part of Wikipedia.

It was fun to review so many sources and we thank everyone for all the hard work! However, if, God forbid, you have discovered an honest-to-goodness mistake in this book, don't hesitate to email my publisher at books@islandportpress.com. We will be sure to correct it in future editions of *Maine Trivia*.

# ABOUT THE AUTHOR

John McDonald is a professional storyteller who has been performing and entertaining audiences in the small towns and big cities of New England for decades. He is an author whose previous books include *A Moose and a Lobster Walk into a Bar* and *Down the Road a Piece: A Storyteller's Guide to Maine*. He also recorded *Ain't He Some Funny* a CD collection of stories and hosts a weekend radio talk show in Portland.

# ABOUT THE ILLUSTRATOR

Mark Ricketts is a Maine-based writer and illustrator who's worked with *Playboy* magazine, McGraw Hill, Dark Horse Comics, *Nickelodeon* magazine, and others. Among other projects, he wrote *Iron Man: The Singularity (Avengers Disassembled)* for Marvel Comics and wrote and illustrated *Nowheresville* for Image Comics.